SECRET SOCIETIES and CRAZY CULTS

METRO BOOKS
New York

An Imprint of Sterling Publishing Co., Inc.
1166 Avenue of the Americas
New York, NY 10036

ISBN 978-1-4351-6763-6

For information about custom editions, special sales, and premium
and corporate purchases, please contact Sterling Special Sales at
800-805-5489 or specialsales@sterlingpublishing.com.

Manufactured in China

2 4 6 8 10 9 7 5 3 1

www.sterlingpublishing.com

Credits: Interior design by Tony Seddon and
cover design by Lindsey Johns

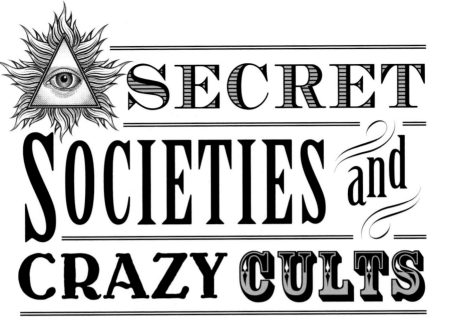

SECRET SOCIETIES and CRAZY CULTS

THE STORY OF SECRET ORDERS THROUGH THE AGES

Jonathan J. Moore

METRO BOOKS
NEW YORK

CONTENTS

INTRODUCTION

I N IRON AGE EUROPE, YOUNG MEN WERE TAKEN TO marshy fenlands with their arms tied behind their backs. On the edge of the solid ground, they were beaten with clubs, stabbed with knives, and garroted. Their blood was then purged from their bodies as the killers slit their throats. The corpses were then pushed under the water, and heavy stones were placed on their chests while wooden withers surrounded the corpses, making sure they stayed underwater. What was the set of beliefs that led to such dreadful killings? Why were gods worshipped with such violence?

A VIOLENT HISTORY

We might imagine that modern societies have moved beyond these barbaric practices, but the evidence is not exactly convincing. Throughout human history notorious cults and secret societies have emerged that have wreaked untold suffering on countless individuals.

During the Middle Ages, the Assassins arose at the crossroads of the Middle East, establishing a reign of terror fueled by a fanatical devotion to Allah and the generous supply of drugs. Drugs also featured heavily in Aztec culture where in one episode the rulers of the Mexica and their vassal kings imbibed a staggering amount of hallucinogenic substances while witnessing the sacrificial killing of 80,000 people over a period of just three days. Just as the Aztecs were shocking the early conquistadors with their brutal human sacrifices, the Spanish Inquisition was torturing and killing fellow Christians with stakes, fire, and the garrote. While the Aztecs sacrificed thousands to their bloodthirsty gods, the Inquisition

LEFT The Catholic Church preached peace, love, and humility. It didn't hesitate to burn anybody who disagreed. Here, a Dutch Anabaptist is consigned to the flames.

ABOVE **A tradition of hundreds of years of martial arts made the Boxers think they were invulnerable.**

killed in the name of Jesus, a prophet who renounced all violence and worldly goods. But the expert stranglers were the Thugs of India, some of whose members were individually responsible for throttling hundreds of innocent travelers.

Several centuries later, in China, the leader of the Taiping, Hong Xiuquan (1814–64), had a series of visions, becoming convinced he was the son of Buddha and Jesus. A decade of carnage followed, in which tens of millions of Chinese died in a series of rebellions. Hong started a trend adopted by later cults. He forbade sexual relations between his followers, while attracting a veritable horde of brides and concubines himself—so many, indeed, that each woman had a number not a name. The Taiping were succeeded by the Boxers—a cult who believed, mistakenly, that martial arts and a red scarf could protect them from Western bullets.

Christianity has created its fair share of crazy cults. Significant among them were the Branch Davidians led by David Koresh (1959–93), a second-rate figure in everything he did except for the ability to brainwash his willing disciples. But at least Koresh didn't shoot first in the battle that wiped out his flock, unlike the demented Reverend Jim Jones (1931–78), who pioneered the one and only mass "revolutionary suicide" by forcing his followers to drink Kool-Aid laced with cyanide.

Doomsday cults have proliferated with the advent of science and technology. Aum Shinrikyo was led by the half-blind Shoko Asahara (1955–), whose longer-term goals included bringing down the Japanese government by mass poisonings. Asahara still sits on Japanese death row for his botched sarin gas attacks on the Japanese subway.

Marshall Applewhite (1931–97) didn't survive his Armageddon. Lacking purpose in life, the members of his cult took their lives to hitch a ride on the Hale–Bopp comet and ascend to another level. The first the world knew of this madness was when police stumbled into the cult's headquarters. Lying on dozens of beds and clad in new Nike trainers and tracksuit pants, they had all swallowed poison before being asphyxiated with the help of a plastic bag over their heads. But at least the members of Applewhite's Heaven's Gate cult went willingly to their deaths; the same can't be said for all of the members of The Solar Temple, many of whom were repeatedly shot or stabbed if they were not keen on being incinerated before moving on to the next stage of enlightenment.

BROTHERHOODS OF HATE

While religious cults have the core task of proving their spiritual superiority over the more common forms of belief, other organizations are brotherhoods of hate, their sole purpose to use violence to subdue their fellow man or exploit them for personal gain. Himmler dressed up the SS as black-clad knights of a new age, but their real role was to eliminate an estimated 10 million European Jews along with 30 million Slavs, murderous desires he concealed beneath the litany of mystical mumbo jumbo espoused by the Thule Society. Similarly, the Ku Klux Klan has kept rising like a phoenix, seeking to imbue white Americans with a hatred for their compatriots of African descent. Repeated efforts by federal governments over many years have tried to eradicate the order, but its members would go into hiding before rising again to threaten society. The KKK and the Nazis used quasi-religious terminology

BELOW **The Ku Klux Klan was like an evil phoenix in American society. It would be supressed only to rise again.**

and quack philosophy to assert their superiority over other races. Criminal brotherhoods such as the Yakuza of Japan and the Sicilian Cosa Nostra use their secret practices to conceal their crimes. Rather than seeking to dominate other racial or social groups, these organizations use or threaten extreme violence to extort money from helpless "civilians."

SHADOWY ORGANIZATIONS

While these cults astound and shock with their fearsome practices there are other, more secret societies which eschew publicity, the shadowy organizations that maybe seek to carry out nefarious actions. The Freemasons and the Illuminati are charged with trying to manipulate the world in their own image. But are these organizations feared only because they are secret? Are they really benign?

Very little is known about many secret societies. This is, of course, because they are secret. Before a member can be initiated they must swear to keep the shadowy goings on well away from the public domain. Sometimes it was necessary for members not to advertise their association. The Bavarian Illuminati and the Rosicrucians were intent on changing society for the better. They sought to challenge the old feudal order where the king or emperor ruled by divine right. Implicit in this challenge was the belief held by these secret societies that the Catholic and Protestant churches were complicit in the subjugation of millions of people through superstition and fear. The Illuminati, in particular, wanted to usher

BELOW The Freemasons have existed for hundreds of years. The initiation process, as seen in this image from ca. 1800, gave access to power and influence.

in a new age based on reason and human rights. They knew that by doing this they would prompt powerful opponents to try and discredit and destroy them. Members well knew the dangers of being branded a "heretic" by the Christian authorities.

Similarly, the Holy Vehm, which flourished in Renaissance Germany, sought to eliminate the criminal activities of robber barons or marauding gangs. In the dead of night, they would capture, try, and punish violent wrongdoers. But if the Holy Vehm's targets got even a whiff of who the vigilantes were, revenge would be swift and bloody. Secrecy meant survival.

Organizations such as the Freemasons and the Independent Order of Odd Fellows began as secret fellowships to ensure that they could give comfort and support to fellow members without being accused of favoritism. These worldwide networks had agreed signs and signals that ensured brothers from different continents could recognize each other. Only now are the veils of secrecy being lifted from these organizations as they seek to remain relevant in the modern world. Not so the Bilderberg Conference—their tremendous influence can only be guessed at.

Enjoy your journey among these crazy cults and secret societies, but no matter how shocking the content, don't doubt for a minute what you're reading. Every word is true.

ABOVE Thousands of heretics were burned alive. Judges had the power to allow the victim to be strangled to death before they went to the stake, but many victims died agonizing deaths, consumed alive by flames.

THE FREEMASONS AND THE ILLUMINATI ARE CHARGED WITH TRYING TO MANIPULATE THE WORLD IN THEIR OWN IMAGE. BUT ARE THESE ORGANIZATIONS FEARED ONLY BECAUSE THEY ARE SECRET? ARE THEY REALLY BENIGN?

CHAPTER 1

DOOMSDAY CULTS

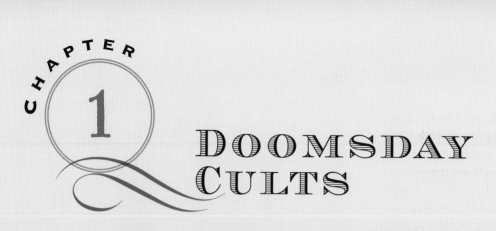

DOOMSDAY CULTS HAVE THINGS IN common beyond the manipulation of their members' belief systems. All believe the end of the world is nigh, and that only their leader can guide them through the coming Apocalypse. They also believe that they are the chosen ones, and all others will die horribly or be damned.

New cults can be termed "survivalists" or "preppers," loose associations of families who remove themselves from major population centers to prepare for an "imminent" collapse of civilization.

THE MILLERITES

During 1843 the inhabitants of various New England parishes, as well as those residing near Pinnacle Hill, Rochester, New York, were treated to a remarkable sight. Night after night thousands of well-meaning Millerites would find the highest place they could and, dressed in flowing white "ascension" robes, raise their arms and gaze upward, waiting to be drawn up to heaven in a celestial white light. Many others wandered in cemeteries, convinced the dead would rise and ascend with them. These fanatics were of course convinced that they alone deserved mercy in the afterlife, and all others should be consigned to an eternity in hellfire.

They were the followers of a Baptist preacher called William Miller (1782–1849), who had prophesied that the second coming of Christ would occur sometime between March in the year 1833 and March 1844. He had based this on a piece of scripture (Daniel 8:14) which stated, the temple of Jerusalem would be rebuilt, and a New Kingdom would emerge in 2,300 days. Biblical scholars often thought that a "day" referred to a year, so Miller surmised that doomsday would occur 2,300 years after the date in 457 BCE when the prophecy was made, and that only those faithful to the true word of Christ would ascend to heaven. So convinced was he of the righteousness of his cause that he traveled all around the United States, giving 4,500 lectures. His supporters created a massive tent that could seat upward of 4,000 people at a time, and this was hauled around with the preacher, lending a carnival-like atmosphere to his dire warnings of impending Armageddon.

Thousands of his believers sold their worldly goods and, equipped only with the clothes on their backs and an ascension robe, headed east, bidding their family and friends goodbye.

By 1844, up to 50,000 may have been baptized into the new creed. But March came and went that year without the "advent" of the heralded new era (another name for the sect was Adventists), much to the consternation of the faithful. Then someone realized that Miller had been using the Christian calendar, not the Jewish one, which allowed believers to

BELOW **This Millerite prophetic time chart sought to prove through "scientific means" that the end of the world was scheduled for 1843.**

extend the "real" date of ascension to April 23rd; but this date, too, passed without divine incident. So one more throw of the celestial dice was made and some fudged figures gave them a new date of October 1844. When the rest of the world's population was not destroyed by brimstone or taken down to the bowels of hell by the time this third date came around, those who had so desired this cleansing of the globe experienced what was called "The Great Disappointment" and left the sect in droves. Having effectively impoverished themselves, the disappointment these acolytes felt at their misplaced beliefs must have been bitter indeed.

Despite so many of the Millerites losing their faith, their prophet still maintained that the day of judgment was just around the corner; only the date had been wrong. Though by this time most considered him more dangerous than good, a small flock of adherents persisted with his cataclysmic visions and established several new churches, one of which was the Seventh-Day Adventists.

BELOW This Millerite has everything he needs to survive the coming holocaust: ham, cigars, brandy, and even a fan to protect him from the flames.

THE SALAMANDER SAFE.

A MILLERITE PREPARING FOR THE 23rd OF APRIL.

Revelations

While the New Testament is filled with many positive messages for mankind, it does have one book which is strikingly at odds with the others— the Book of Revelation. While most theologists see this book as a metaphor for internal struggle, others see it as a prophetic vision of the horrible fate that awaits most of mankind. The book is full of dreadful visons: a holy sword descending from the heavens, angels clearing sinners off the earth, armies numbering 200 million men, earthquakes, flaming mountains crashing into the sea, locusts, dragons, seven-headed monsters.

The beauty of having so many visions is that Christian doomsday cults such as the Millerites and the Branch Davidians can pick and choose whatever passage they want to prove that the end of the world is coming.

Christianity is not the only religion that believes in such cataclysms. Islamic fanatics look forward to the Day of Judgment when the Mahdi (the Guided One) and Jesus will appear on white horses to fight the False Messiah. Buddhists believe that in 5,000 years seven suns will destroy the earth. Hindus wait with anticipation for Vishnu to descend, also on a white horse, to end the Age of Devils.

No one is sure who wrote the Book of Revelation, but it appears that it was written somewhere aound 60–70 CE. It has been interpreted as largely an attack on the oppressive Roman empire. This was during the reign of Nero (37–68 CE), who enjoyed persecuting Christians. The number of the Antichrist, 666, is a reference to Nero in an ancient Hebrew code known as Gematria, and 'The seven heads are seven mountains' refers to the seven hills of Rome.

RIGHT This 1086 manuscript shows the seven-headed monster that the Book of Revelation declares will usher in the Apocalypse. Only true believers were expected to survive.

THE SHAKERS

Unlike most doomsday cults the Shakers weren't obsessed with death and destruction; they got off on song, dance, and artwork. Nevertheless, they did believe they were the chosen people and thought that the end of the world was coming. But the end of the cult did not come with cataclysmic Armageddon and the return of Christ the Savior; Shakers believed in celibacy and died out through natural attrition.

Emerging during the mid-18th century in England and America, they were originally called the "United Society of Believers in Christ's Second Appearing," convinced that through the intervention of spiritual women Christ would appear on the millennium and cleanse the world. They believed that God spoke through them, and this manifested in frenetic dancing and speaking in tongues, practices from which they earned the name "Shakers."

In 1770, Mother Ann Lee was proclaimed a second Christ, declaring that she had a direct line to God and to Adam and Eve, on whose advice she established the rule that all members of her cult must renounce sex and marriage. For some reason, this idea attracted thousands of adherents, and by the 1840s there were many Shaker communities scattered throughout America. Sexual

BELOW **Rows of Shakers dancing in a meeting hall in New York. Frenetic dancing and religious ecstasy replaced sexual relations, which were forbidden in the cult.**

ecstasy was replaced by spiritual fulfillment as thousands of young women and men expressed joy through dance and art.

By the late-19th century numbers had begun to decline, but the cult's death knell came in the mid-20th century when American Federal laws forbade religious organizations from adopting orphans—the only way the celibate cult could maintain membership.

Today there are only two known Shakers, although the cult's artwork and furnishings are highly prized by collectors.

ABOVE **The Book of Revelation has so many creatures of dread that its dire warnings can be interpreted in any way that a doomsday cult sees fit.**

THEY BELIEVED THAT GOD SPOKE THROUGH THEM, AND THIS MANIFESTED IN FRENETIC DANCING AND SPEAKING IN TONGUES, PRACTICES FROM WHICH THEY EARNED THE NAME "SHAKERS."

THE TAIPING

Hong Xiuquan demonstrated how even the most insignificant individual can rise to cult leader and alter history. Hong declared himself Jesus Christ's brother and set off a revolution in China that almost toppled the Manchu dynasty, leading to years of warfare that may have claimed in excess of 50 million lives. Like many doomsday cultists, Hong thought the End of Days was approaching along with the Messiah, but in this case proclaimed himself to be the Messiah.

Hong came from a small ethnic minority called the Hakka. Culturally different to the mainstream Han Chinese and their Manchu rulers, they nevertheless tried to rise within Chinese society. The path for many to gain respect was to join the civil service by demonstrating an understanding of Confucian ideology.

Hong was the youngest son of a poor family but showed promise and was sponsored to sit the civil service entrance exams. Praised and doted upon by his family, after passing the preliminary exams, he nevertheless failed the much more demanding imperial exams three times. The third failure brought on an emotional collapse that plunged him into a fevered delirium that lasted for weeks.

When Hong emerged from his delirium he had a new career path—to become a prophet and son of God. His was a classic end-of-the-world dream where an old man, whom he later

ABOVE **Taiping rebels at Shanghai, China, in 1853–54. Millions of peasants were turned into a fanatical crusading army determined to create a heavenly kingdom on earth.**

identified as God, gave Hong a sword to rid the world of evil demons; moreover, a middle-aged man, later identified by Hong as Jesus Christ, also gave him invaluable advice on how to cleanse the world of the same source of trouble.

In tandem with his good friend Feng Yunshan (1815–52), Hong founded the Society of God Worshippers and began to proselytize. But the doctrine of the new society was based not on humility and peace but on smiting the enemy—particularly the hated Manchu rulers. The growing cult attracted thousands of poor peasants to the cause, and soon a huge irregular army was rampaging through the countryside destroying any opposition.

Hong proclaimed his kingdom the Taiping Tianguo (Heavenly Kingdom of Great Peace) on January 1, 1851 and proclaimed himself the "Heavenly King." He began implementing a radical agenda, abolishing harsh taxes and giving all the conquered land to poor peasants. Manchu administrators were slaughtered and wealthy individuals were lucky to escape with their lives. Alcohol, gambling, foot binding, and the use of opium were all banned. Women were proclaimed equal with men and Hong's armies swelled to up to a million, allowing the Taiping to extend their reach across almost a third of the provinces of China. Rewards and punishments were divinely ordained: any soldier who died in the service of the Taiping was guaranteed immediate access to heaven, while any who fled were condemned to an eternity in hell.

Over time Hong became increasingly delusional and decidedly hypocritical. While sexual relations were banned among ordinary members, Hong and his lieutenants were allowed to create enormous harems. Once Nanjing had been captured he disappeared into an enormous palace to be pleasured by his harem and to smoke opium. Like all cult leaders, a different set of rules applied to him and his inner circle.

While he dreamed great thoughts and sated his desires, the Manchu were using foreign expertise to launch a counterattack. Villages, towns, and cities were destroyed by the avenging government troops, with at least 20 million, and possibly as many as 50 million, dying in the subsequent re-conquest. This was total war and both sides used scorched-earth policies to try to deprive their enemies of supplies, with an estimated 600 large towns leveled in the process. In 1862, Nanjing was surrounded by government troops, but Hong refused to lay in supplies, being sure that God would intervene to meet the Taiping's needs. Unsurprisingly, God didn't intervene, and in 1864 the self-appointed Heavenly King committed suicide. Thereafter, the Manchu took a dreadful revenge against the Hakka minority, with hundreds of thousands massacred and their language and culture almost totally destroyed.

BELOW **Only with help from "foreign devils" were the Manchu able to supress the Taiping. Millions of Chinese perished.**

DAVID KORESH AND THE BRANCH DAVIDIANS

Many cults appear to the outside world to be fairly peaceful. Their members may be considered a bit strange or otherworldly, but overall such groups appear unified and content with their lot. But this is not always the case, as beyond many a united front vicious fights for supremacy among cult members may well be taking place.

Never was this more true than with the Branch Davidians, a sect which in the course of the 1980s was gradually taken over by Vernon Howell, a mediocre musician whose only real talents were self-promotion and a love of guns.

The Seventh Day Adventists (referred to simply as Adventists), as we have seen, are a Christian cult that grew out of the Millerites, in a similar way looking forward to the Second Coming of Christ (the Advent of Christ). The Davidian Seventh Day Adventists (Davidians) are an ancillary group that split off from the main Adventist movement in the 1930s, and they in turn further splintered in 1955, when a new offshoot called the Branch Davidians (The Branch) was created. While this is all pretty confusing, the Davidians and the Branch both believe that they are living in the time of the Second Coming—that Jesus Christ's return is just around the corner.

The Young Religious Zealot

Vernon Howell was born in August 1959 to his teenage single mother, Bonnie Sue Clark, and a father by the name of Bobby Wayne Howell. Howell was soon missing in action, and Vernon was brought up by a succession of maladjusted relatives. Vernon performed poorly in school and was often in special classes. He dropped out of junior high, and it was not until his early twenties that he discovered his real talent—an ability to select passages from the Bible and use them to get his way. He had earlier joined his mother's branch of the Adventists and fallen in love with the pastor's daughter. He miraculously "found" a line out of Isaiah that declared "… none should want for a mate," and using this divine proclamation tried to convince the pastor to hand over his virgin daughter. The pastor could obviously spot a deranged charlatan a mile off and gave Vernon his marching orders.

Vernon shifted his deluded gaze to another sect and in 1983 joined the Branch Davidians. While a weak student at school throughout his adolescence, he had gradually turned from an easy-going child into a religious zealot. He spent much of his spare time reading the Bible. It turned out he had a photographic memory and could recite lengthy passages of the Old Testament at will. He was able to use this encyclopedic knowledge of a text to win any theological argument by turning biblical passages into verbal weapons to prove his point.

New Leader, New Name

The Branch Davidians were harmless cranks left to their own devices in a compound located at Waco, Texas. When Howell joined them he immediately challenged the authority of the assumed heir to the leadership of the group, George B. Roden. Not only was his knowledge of scripture superior to Roden's, but he began a relationship with Roden's mother, at that time the leader of the sect and its guiding light over several decades.

Sister Louise Roden was well into her sixties by this time but Vernon didn't seem to mind. Both George Roden and his mother proclaimed themselves to be the Messiah, but Howell thought he was getting closer to God by entering a relationship with the old woman.

Both men began to gather followers for the inevitable showdown that would occur when Sister Roden passed on. Howell's claims became more strident as he gathered support by claiming to be the only man on earth who truly understood the word of God. He spoke of a divine revelation he had had while on a trip to Israel,

ABOVE **Throughout history many prophets have declared themselves to be the resurrected Christ. This allows them to assume total power over their devoted followers.**

ABOVE **Vernon Howell, aka David Koresh, would harangue his flock for hour after hour.**

which revealed that he was the Lamb of God. Only he could open the seventh seal and set off the Apocalypse. He, Vernon Howell, would then lead the 144,000 chosen folk into the new age of Christ.

While this may seem crazy to many, Howell was in fact probably saner than George B. Roden. When the matriarch finally died, the real power struggle began with Roden deciding to assert his spiritual superiority over the young usurper by staging a competitive resurrection. Figuring that he could bring a long-deceased member of the cult back to life a lot quicker than Vernon, he threw down the gauntlet to his rival, declaring that whoever raised the dead person more quickly would be acknowledged as the "living prophet."

While most people might think this behavior pretty unhinged, Roden's supporters embraced the challenge with a will. Armed with picks and shovels they descended on the compound's cemetery and dug up the coffin of poor old Anna Hughes, who

20 years earlier had died a spinster at the ripe old age of 84. They placed a flag with the Star of David over the coffin and began praying and hollering for divine intervention to bring the poor old woman back to life.

Howell wasn't crazy enough at that point to be taken in by such a scheme and instead took a heavily armed party of his supporters to seize the coffin so that George could be charged with unlawfully interfering with the dead. They were found out and a firefight erupted, with semi-automatic weapons and high-powered rifles being used as the supposedly peaceful cult members tried to sort out their differences. The local sheriffs turned up and arrested the gun-toting Davidians, and it seemed that Howell and his supporters were in for a long stretch in a penitentiary.

But this was Texas. Vernon and his supporters were hauled before a judge on charges of attempted murder, but all the charges were dismissed. This was a pyrrhic victory for George B. Roden, who had been wounded in the firefight, as his increasingly bizarre behavior saw him jailed and then committed to a sanatorium for the mentally ill in 1989.

With this turn of events Vernon Howell moved in and began to bend the once peaceful Branch Davidians to his will. The following year, 1990, he changed his name to David Koresh, which in itself was a telling indicator of his motivations. The name David of course ties him in with the royal line of Israel's rulers, the implication being that he was the new Christ. Koresh has multiple meanings, one of which is a variation on the great Persian emperor Cyrus, the destroyer of Babylon. Another interpretation is that it stands for "destroyer"—implying that in his deluded imaginings he renamed himself Christ the Destroyer.

Consolidating Power

Koresh's subsequent actions over the course of the next few years fit the pattern of classic cult manipulation. He became the arbiter of all that was good and evil; the community became entirely dependent upon him, and his power over the poor misled cult members became total.

Initially, neighbors on adjoining ranches noticed some good things when the new management took over. Ramshackle buildings were torn down and piles of junk and old cars were hauled away. Many of the larger buildings were refurbished and an impressive new tower was built. However, any person with a military background might have seen the sinister implications of these improvements. The larger buildings were actually being reinforced with concrete, making them impervious to small arms fire. The tower gave Koresh an unimpeded view around the district and allowed the cult to identify threats from miles away. By clearing out the debris and cutting down trees the cult was given a free field of fire if needed. Less obvious was the work going on underground. Water wells were dug and an old bus was sunk into the earth to

MOST OF THE MEMBERS WERE CONVINCED TO SELL ALL OF THEIR
ASSETS OR SIGN OVER THEIR SOCIAL SERVICES PAYMENTS TO THE
NEW LEADER. THOSE WHO HELD DOWN JOBS OUTSIDE THE COMPOUND
WOULD BE ENCOURAGED TO TITHE 90 PERCENT OF THEIR INCOME TO
THE BRANCH, AND ALL CONTACT WITH OUTSIDE FAMILY AND FRIENDS
WAS ACTIVELY DISCOURAGED.

form a rudimentary bunker. Many tunnels were dug to connect the entire building
complex with an interlinked series of blockhouses and fortifications. Below the
largest building was a large subterranean weapons store with an armored door, an
arsenal to which only Koresh had a set of keys.

At the same time as the new leader was changing the physical infrastructure of
what became known as "Ranch Apocalypse," Koresh was also beginning to mold the
minds of his followers. They were already well regulated and used to long hours
working with few creature comforts, and Koresh built on this foundation to ensure
growing obedience. He was in control of the foods eaten by cult members and
ensured they were always hungry. A light breakfast was followed by a light lunch,
with dinner often non-existent. Frequently, they had to fast, although Koresh could
dole out extra rations for his favorites or as rewards to disempower the rest.

Most of the members were convinced to sell all of their assets or sign over their
social services payments to the new leader. Those who held down jobs outside the
compound would be encouraged to tithe 90 percent of their income to the Branch,
and all contact with outside family and friends was actively discouraged. This new
income stream was not used to fund good charitable events or programs; on the
contrary, Koresh set himself up as an arms dealer. It became common to hear the
sound of automatic gunfire coming from the compound, as all members of the cult
were given weapons training. This was mingled with the crump of hand grenades
detonating and even satchel charges being blown up. Heavy-caliber machine guns
were purchased and, in a final sign that the cult was becoming more of a prison than
a religious institution, armed guards were often seen patrolling the perimeter—as
much to keep cult members in as intruders out.

The family units of members were broken up with separate dormitories for men,
women, and children. Wives were not to consort with husbands, and children would
be put in the care of other adults—a classic cult leader's ploy to ensure that the only
meaningful relationship disciples had was with him.

Just like Jim Jones of the Peoples Temple, Koresh loved the sound of his own voice and would summon his tired followers at any time of the day or night to listen to his long-winded dissertations on the Bible. Koresh often snacked on ice cream, or sucked on soda, while his half-starving congregation looked on. What was perhaps worse, he would summon the entire flock to listen to him ripping out some power chords on his electric guitar. His playing was described as discordant, out of tune, and without rhythm. The poor cult members must have thanked God when he finally relented, often after hours of bad music, and let them go to bed. At other times Koresh would stage movie marathons for his flock. Not Cecil B. DeMille's (1881–1959) *The Ten Commandments*, but violent movies such as *Platoon* and *Apocalypse Now*.

ABOVE **Koresh sought to recruit cult members from around the globe. International members, such as those pictured here, presented a friendly face to the outside world.**

Being a bad musician as well as being a fanatic Bible thumper is bad enough, but soon Koresh added a less forgivable sin—he became a pedophile and rapist. With typical guru-style doublethink Koresh declared that he was the Messiah partly due to his understanding that he was a sinner. By sinning he was able to understand how corrosive drinking, cussing, and womanizing were.

A Culture of Fear

Koresh decided that the new Kingdom of David needed to be populated by the seeds of his holy loins—24 offspring were required to be the ruling elders in the new age. It was their responsibility to determine exactly who could continue to live after the Apocalypse. All women within the cult (and indeed the entire world) became his property. This began with single women, but soon married women were summoned to the prophet's bed.

A phrase from the 45th psalm details anointing the head of a king with "oil of gladness," a phrase that Koresh interpreted as vaginal secretions, which in his mind gave the green light to the unhindered sexual access he demanded of his many wives. Admittedly, some couples saw this as just a step too far and left, but most submitted to this new outrage. The last barrier of morality was overcome. Visitors or family members of cultists who visited the compound—they became rare and rarer—noticed that girls as young as ten were wearing the Star of David. While this six-pointed star has meant many things, in the Branch's eyes it indicated that these girls were slated to be Koresh's bed mates. Outside the compound Koresh purchased a large house, within which was deposited his harem of young mothers and children. Members learned to fear the Messiah. Any child who crossed him or refused instruction could be beaten until their buttocks bled. Some were locked in small subterranean cells until they were deemed to have learnt their lesson.

ABOVE *Four Horsemen of the Apocalypse*, by Albrecht Durer, 1497–98. Doomsday Cult leaders seek to welcome the Four Horsemen of the Apocalypse to exterminate everybody on earth except their devotees.

LEFT Vernon Wayne Howell with his first wife Rachel and their son Cyrus. He soon demanded more "wives" and wanted to sire 24 children.

Many cult leaders keep their flocks in line by building a culture of fear, a fear of outsiders and the concept of "us versus them." Koresh proved to be a past master at this and created an atmosphere of impending doom. The last showdown with the unrighteous Philistines was fast approaching. Martyrdom at the hands of the unbelievers was to be welcomed; resurrection and a place at David's side would be guaranteed. Koresh used all of his skills as an orator to prepare his followers for the coming conflict. He would take waverers aside and, using his full charismatic and charming powers of persuasion, banish their last doubts. Gospel sessions went on for hours, warning of the evil

ABOVE Two armed agents of the ATF form a roadblock near the shooting scene in Waco, Texas.

intentions and tempting offers of those on the outside. Few of his sleep-deprived semi-starving flock could resist. As one former member said, "You had moments when you were resentful and wanted to rebel, but you knew you were rebelling against the word of God."

Koresh and his more devoted followers, including his well-armed retinue of "Mighty Men," began to talk of the stark virtues of suicide—if they couldn't fight for the Lamb of God, they could at least die for him. Even youngsters were taught the necessity to be ready for suicide. One young cult member recalled that Koresh himself explained to the children that it was best to stick a barrel of a gun in their mouth before firing. If it was held to the side of the head, he explained, it was too easy to inflict only a superficial wound.

Not everyone swallowed this garbage. It seems that in the final hours of the siege at Waco, some women and children sought to flee. They were gunned down.

The Siege

Koresh's increasingly bizarre behavior began to alert the authorities that all was not well in "Ranch Apocalypse." Various law enforcement bureaus were beginning to take an interest, including the ATF (Bureau of Alcohol, Tobacco, Firearms and Explosives) and the local sheriffs. Koresh himself was aware of the heightened interest, partly due to some damaging newspaper reports. This led him to declare that Armageddon was about to happen in Waco, and he summoned members from England and Australia to marshal his resources for the coming conflict.

The "Lamb of God" was well prepared. By this time the compound was stocked with boxes of hand grenades and over 300 weapons. These included AK-47 assault rifles, Beretta semi-automatic pistols, and 9 mm Glock handguns. Men and women mounted a 24-hour guard around the compound, and so wary were the cultists that they went about their everyday activities with a loaded weapon or a string of hand grenades by their side. Perhaps most troubling were the incendiary devices scattered throughout the main buildings of the compound, waiting to be ignited to reduce the buildings to a deadly conflagration.

A tinder box of sexual abuse, religious fanaticism, heavily armed cultists, and Koresh's apocalyptic visions was waiting to be ignited on the plains of Texas. A botched ATF raid would light that fuse.

Several reasons were given for the ATF's decision to lead a military-style operation against a compound filled with heavily armed religious zealots. Some suppose that it was to get extra funding from Congress with a media triumph, while the ATF maintains it was standard operating procedure. Whatever the motivations, it was a colossal blunder that resulted in more than one hundred dead. Koresh often went into town, to bars and guitar shops. With a modicum of patience and planning, the ATF might well have been able to seize him well away from his fanatical followers and lethal arsenal.

Instead, on the morning of February 28, 1993, hundreds of ATF personnel armed with flak jackets and semi-automatic weapons headed off to Ranch Apocalypse in a large convoy. Flying above were attack helicopters borrowed from the National Guard. Shipped in large trucks and even some armored personnel carriers, the ATF detail approached the compound like it was a military combat unit. The operation had been planned for eight months and for several weeks the agents had been practicing their assault tactics on a mock-up of the Davidian buildings. As they dismounted from their trucks and began the assault, they were more gung-ho than

MEN AND WOMEN MOUNTED A 24-HOUR GUARD AROUND THE COMPOUND, AND SO WARY WERE THE CULTISTS THAT THEY WENT ABOUT THEIR EVERYDAY ACTIVITIES WITH A LOADED WEAPON OR A STRING OF HAND GRENADES BY THEIR SIDE.

John Wayne. The assault teams divided into three parties: one to seize the armory by going through some upstairs windows; another to seize Koresh and his "Mighty Men;" and another to protect the women and children.

As the second team stormed the main entrance yelling, "Federal Agents! We have a search warrant," the double doors were opened. There stood Koresh. He slammed the doors shut and all of a sudden the entire compound was engulfed in gunfire. The agents were caught in a perfect storm. Cultists fired out of windows and even through walls to take down the ATF agents. As they tumbled into cover hand grenades were lobbed at them, blasting the agents senseless and inflicting bloody shrapnel wounds. Cult snipers popped up from all parts of the compound, emerging from the warren of tunnels and firing from the recently built four-story tower that dominated the area. Many of the ATF were veterans from the military, and could make out the heavy staccato sound of a .50 cal machine gun. These 12 mm bullets could cut through any light cover and could even reach the media vans parked over half a mile away.

BELOW **The fire takes hold during the FBI siege at Waco, Texas. Koresh's prophecy of a flaming Armageddon had come true.**

The fact that the media were there shows how the ATF had managed a classic snafu. The original intention had been to raid

first thing in the morning when all of the male cultists would be in the fields working while the rest were in the chapel praying. However, Koresh received various tipoffs that the raid was coming, and even the local and national media knew something was up. They had driven up in the pre-dawn light to set up cameras and sound gear. Given such ample warning of impending Armageddon, Koresh made sure his cult members were armed and ready. In the ensuing firefight, four ATF men died and another 16 were seriously injured. A similar number of cultists died in the initial battle, which went on for several hours until the ATF finally pulled out.

Negotiators managed to get in touch with the compound to arrange a ceasefire. Koresh was wounded but would listen to reason. Tellingly, the key message he sought to communicate was his role in unlocking the seventh seal. Even with a gunshot in his side, small arms fire ricocheting through the building, and 100 enraged cultists determined to shoot off as much ammo as possible, the thing uppermost in his mind was to have a biblical discussion with the local FBI.

Apart from some minor skirmishes, the conflict settled down into a siege operation that lasted from February 28th to April 19th. M113 armored personnel carriers were vulnerable to .50 cal fire and were withdrawn, to be replaced by M2 Bradley Fighting Vehicles that formed an armored ring around the compound. The FBI took over and immediately instituted talks to de-escalate the situation.

It seemed at first they were dealing with a rational man. Elderly and very young cult members were allowed to leave. A deal was brokered whereby Koresh would have access to national radio to broadcast a one-hour sermon before surrendering all, including himself, to the authorities.

Euphoria gripped the Federal agents as well as the besieged Davidians. Buses were drawn up to take them away while the cultists packed their meager possessions. But it was not to be. Koresh got a message from God telling him to stay put and await further developments. As one frustrated FBI negotiator said, "You can't argue with God."

Let it Burn

In fact, the "Lamb of God" would not compromise any further. All of the children had left the compound except for his offspring, his future judges of the Apocalypse. To hand them over would indicate that he was willing to renounce his entire theology. In Koresh's warped imaginings the remaining children shared his DNA—God's DNA—and could not be handed over to the forces of darkness.

The FBI escalated their assault on the compound not with physical violence but with psychological warfare. All night monstrous sounds blared through the Davidian grounds at maximum volume. These included the sounds of sheep and livestock being slaughtered as well as discordant music. These tactics were combined with floodlights and lasers turning night into day. The aim was to wear down resistance, but it had the opposite effect. In fact, the FBI played into Koresh's hands. He had convinced his followers that they were "God's Marines" fighting the agents of the Apocalypse, and these actions by the FBI proved his prophecies right and hardened the cult's resolve to fight until the end.

Koresh could not surrender and never would. The longer the siege dragged on—it was the longest in US history up to that time—the stronger he became. Not so the Clinton administration. As 51 days ticked over, the President decided that the FBI had to act or else he would lose face. Once again they played right into Koresh's hands.

For months the FBI had been considering smoking the besieged cultists out of the compound using tear gas canisters and specially adapted, heavily armored Combat Engineer Vehicles or CEVs. On the morning of April 19th, two CEVs approached the compound and ripped holes in the sides of the larger structures before injecting tear gas to try to force the Davidians out. Loudspeakers blared, urging them to leave the compound, saying the FBI would not fire. None came out and not until six hours later, around midday, did the Davidians act.

Koresh began the final act of his deluded fantasies. Incendiary points had been scattered throughout the buildings, and now his most faithful followers set them alight. Small fires broke out and within a matter of minutes the compound was ablaze. Nine cultists staggered out but the rest were caught in the resulting inferno, consumed by the leaping fires or trapped underground by falling debris and concrete rafters.

Others were killed by Koresh's "Mighty Men." Five children had stab wounds to their chests and one had had his head beaten in. Some members were burned beyond recognition but others had bullet wounds in their back indicating they had been executed while trying to flee.

Koresh was found with his closest supporter. Both had single shots to the head. Which one died first is not known but Koresh had not had the courage to die in the flames of his beloved Apocalypse and, unlike his betrayed followers, had taken the easy way out. God's son was a coward.

Seventy-six Branch Davidians died in this final act, following the five killed in the initial firefight. Twenty-two of the victims were children.

DOOMSDAY PREPPERS

In what is a particularly American phenomenon, a new group has emerged in society. They call themselves "preppers" or "survivalists" and their aim is to survive an event that leads to the total collapse of civilization.

Christian doomsayers should consider themselves lucky, as the only threat they envisage is the return of the Anti-Christ and the battle between Satan and Jesus. Preppers have much more to worry about. Things to fear are: atomic war and the resulting radioactive fallout, biological warfare, chemical warfare, continent-wide natural disasters, global natural disasters, comet strikes, economic collapse due to peak oil being reached, foreign invasion, an intrusive government coming into power that is determined to strip citizens of guns and civil liberties, and worldwide drought. (No doubt at the back of many preppers' minds is the secret desire for an alien invasion or a zombie plague.)

These concerns are very real in the minds of survivalists, and many take extreme steps to guarantee their future safety which exceed the demands of even the craziest cults. Many stockpile huge amounts of foods, water, and medicine.

Of course, these items have use-by dates, so the cost of keeping these necessities fresh can be huge. Many remove themselves to wilderness areas and build fortified compounds which include stringent security measures, and equip themselves with camouflage kit and night-vision goggles. All family members are taught survival skills that include gathering wild foods, obtaining fresh water, and, of course, fighting off hostiles who will be after their precious accrued resources.

Any prepper equips himself with a fair and foul weather armoury. The AK-47 is the most sought-after weapon due to its robust reliability and well-proven stopping power. Crossbows and axes are also desired as effective combat weapons that require minimal maintenance. In common with many cults, preppers tend to remove themselves from their extended families as their world view becomes more paranoid and fantasy replaces reality. But then again, they may prove to be right!

RIGHT Crossbows are weapons favored by doomsday preppers because they require minimal maintenance.

AUM SHINRIKYO

By the mid-1990s the Japanese doomsday cult Aum Shinrikyo (Supreme Truth) had assets in excess of 200 million US dollars and a working turnover estimated at 1 billion dollars per annum. The semi-blind cult leader Shoko Asahara was determined to use these assets to survive what he thought was coming, namely, Armageddon. He had confidently predicted to his inner circle of fanatical worshippers that it was rapidly approaching. By 1996, he insisted, the world would plunge into a holocaust like no other, and only Asahara and his devoted supporters would survive. And if the global superpowers didn't trigger the cataclysmic nuclear event, Asahara was going to use his assets to bring it about.

His real name was Chizuo Matsumoto, and he was born in 1955 into the humblest of all possible backgrounds. The son of an impoverished mat-weaver, he was one of six siblings in a household in the unremarkable village of Yatushiro. Suffering from a poor diet while in utero Matsumoto suffered infantile glaucoma and was blind in one eye with vastly diminished vision in the other; at the age of six he was enrolled in a school for the blind in the nearby city of Kumamoto. Once in the school Matsumoto found that he was unique among the other students in having some vestigial vision. While others would have used this advantage for doing good deeds, even at the age of six Matsumoto was showing his true colors. He manipulated his peers, solicited bribes, bullied them, and used violence and an evil temper to get his way. Even many years later, his classmates remembered one thing about the young Matsumoto—he was a bully. He was also, due to his various schemes, a rich bully and left high school with a healthy bank balance.

In 1977 the young man went to Tokyo and set himself up as an acupuncturist and herbal healer. He also began to dabble in a range of Eastern religions and in 1984 set up Aum Inc., a small meditation workshop which also sold health remedies and literature. Early members of this organization remembered Aum Inc. as a fun organization to belong to, and the membership soon grew to 3,000. But it did not take long for the guru's darker side to take over.

Matsumoto toured extensively and caught the Dalai Lama unawares in a "photo bomb," using this photo to tout himself as a spiritual practitioner on a level equal to the revered Tibetan leader. With the wind of this publicity behind him Matsumoto began to stretch his wings, allowing his dark fantasies to assume greater prominence within the cult. In 1986 he proclaimed that he had reached nirvana and the following year the cult was renamed Aum Shinrikyo at the same time as he changed his own name, formally, to Shoko Asahara. Two crucial changes then occurred: a large tract of land was bought in Fujinomiya, which would soon become a massive compound,

RIGHT **Shoko Asahara, who founded the Aum Shinrikyo cult, hid a burning hatred of mankind behind a benevolent exterior.**

and the cult's purpose altered from personal salvation to one that would save the world from demonic energies.

As his delusional visions darkened, it became necessary for the cult to grow. Good-looking young cult members traveled throughout Japan snaring possible members. They used sex, propaganda, and even drugs to recruit isolated and vulnerable Japanese. These recruitment groups became more sinister and would eventually use violence and intimidation to recruit members and force them to sign over their worldly goods. The other necessity was huge amounts of money. Asahara's first Japanese business had been closed when the authorities had jailed him for peddling orange peel soaked in alcohol as a wonder medicine. But that fraud was tiny compared to the huge sums he extorted from the thousands of increasingly brainwashed cult members.

BELOW Cult member wearing a "Perfect Salvation Headset." Members believed the headset allowed them to tune directly into Shoko Asahara's brainwaves.

The guru's bathwater sold for hundreds of dollars a pint; his followers were expected to drink it and inherit his wisdom. A small vial of his blood was more expensive, although not as much as a vial of his DNA (semen). Small badges containing the master's "energy" could be bought for a thousand dollars and in the most amazing scam of all, for thousands of dollars a month subjects could rent a "Perfect Salvation Headset." This bizarre-looking piece of headwear was covered in electrodes and wires and was supposed to plug the wearer straight into the guru's superior thought patterns. Cult members became so reliant on these phony contraptions that they could experience nervous breakdowns if the devices were removed.

The lay believers made up the majority of Aum's membership and they were royally fleeced. All kinds of expensive courses were offered in the cause of enlightenment, such as an "Advanced Correspondence Course for Supernatural Powers" costing thousands of dollars, but all that was enlightened were loyal believers' wallets. Unbelievably, the lay believers, who carried on their daily lives as normal, were more fortunate than the "monastics." These full-time followers lived in Aum compounds and renounced all their worldly goods, handing them over to the cult. Property, bank accounts, and inheritances were all given to Aum, and they were only allowed to bring a case of clothes with them. Once in the clutches of the organization, they were forced to work around the clock in Aum industries, whether it was printing or submachine-gun manufacturing. Given a thin starvation diet of steamed vegetables, they slept in crowded single-sex dormitories. Sexual contact was forbidden as all female monastics belonged to the guru. Constant indoctrination was the order of the day, and all contact with the outside world was strictly forbidden.

Many monastics realized the fearful mistake they had made, but found it impossible to leave. The Fujinomiya compound became an armed camp and was ringed by high barbed-wire fences patrolled 24/7 by armed guards. If anyone did manage to escape, specially trained kidnap teams hunted them down and brought them back. Word began to get out about these dark practices, as Asahara moved from dangerous crank to murderer.

A Mission to Kill

The first known victim of Aum Shinrikyo was a 14-month-old baby. In November 1989, the cult's "special action squad," snuck into the family bedroom of lawyer Tsutsumi Sakamoto (who was working on a class action lawsuit against Aum Shinrikyo) and killed his infant with a lethal injection, before turning the needle fatally on his wife and then the lawyer himself. But another run-in with the law would take the cult from assassins of a single family to outright mass murderers.

Asahara's cult had amassed a fearsome array of deadly weapons and devices. Scattered around Japan were compounds packed with cult paraphernalia.

ABOVE Japanese lawyer Tsutsumi Sakamoto and his family. All three were murdered on Asahara's orders and buried in different locations around Japan.

A disassembled Soviet-era attack helicopter was awaiting reconstruction. A state-of-the-art metalworking factory named "Clear Stream Temple" was close to the main compound in the shadow of Mount Fuji. It was filled with furnaces and lathes with more than a hundred staff turning out parts for Kalashnikov semi-automatic firearms. Materials to make Kevlar armored vests were stockpiled nearby. Aum had invested in state-of-the-art laser technology and was experimenting with advanced optics to turn these lasers into deadly weapons. Some of the cult boffins were experimenting with huge microwave ovens to develop lethal proton beams. While this was one of the more far-fetched schemes, the microwaves had another function—to dispose of dead cult members by turning them into brown sludge.

The Russian outposts of Asahara's organization were even more ambitious, busy trolling the Soviet Union seeking to purchase anti-aircraft missiles, T-72 tanks, and even nuclear weapons. Ex-special forces military personnel trained cult cadres in offensive and defensive weapons tactics. In a few short years Shoko Asahara had thousands of brainwashed cult members all willing to die for their guru.

More deadly than this scary assortment of doomsday paraphernalia was Aum's massive chemical and germ warfare establishment. Botulism toxin is one of the deadliest substances known to man. As a bacterium it comes in several toxic strains, with Type A being the deadliest. It is 16 million times more toxic than strychnine, with only radioactive isotopes such as those used by Soviet assassins being more deadly. A human can be killed by one millionth of a gram. Mild forms create food poisoning, but in its most lethal forms it is a vicious neurotoxin that prevents basic messages being sent to your nervous system; the heart forgets to beat and the lungs are unable to breathe.

The beauty of such a weapon for Aum was that it takes almost a whole day for symptoms to emerge. Metropolises such as Tokyo could be inundated with the lethal agent and nobody would know until it was much too late. Aum not only had access to several pounds of this deadly powder but also possessed a special device for spraying a solution of the botulism toxin. In April 1990, members of the cult drove through the center of Tokyo and around the government district, all the while spraying a colorless mist of the deadly gas. The aim was to destroy the government and step in to pick up the pieces.

This first experiment with botulism came to naught, as millions of Japanese went about their daily business. The lethal bug is an anaerobic pathogen, so was killed as soon as it was exposed to oxygen; fortunately for hundreds of thousands of Japanese, Aum didn't have a means of delivering it to the intended victims. But another attempt was made in June 1993 during the Crown Prince's wedding, when Asahara himself rode in the van that sought to wipe out the royal family and hundreds of visiting diplomats.

Once again this mad scheme failed, but Asahara remained undaunted. A new bio lab was established in an eight-story building in the heart of Tokyo, with the aim of growing and unleashing anthrax on the innocent Japanese residents. *Bacillus anthracis* is the Latin name for this deadly bacterium. This nasty spore can lie dormant in soils for years before being ingested, inhaled, or entering the bloodstream through, say, a cut. As a powder it is a lethal agent. Aum was perhaps inspired by an incident in 2001, in which a series of letters containing the deadly spores were anonymously sent to US federal authorities. Government almost ground to a halt as the mysterious letters killed five and infected many more. Those who died suffered a horrible death. Several days after inhaling the spores they developed a mild cold which then turned into a flu characterized by vomiting and high fever. As the bacterium overwhelms the body's defenses the skin turns black while blisters break out. The blood itself turns almost black, the lungs fill with fluid, and the body shuts down due to lack of oxygen.

Aum's ambitions were much greater than killing five workers. On the rooftop of his headquarters a large industrial sprayer was built with a powerful fan attached to generators and for four days steam filled with anthrax spores poured out over central

Tokyo. Aum scientists wearing airtight biohazard suits stoked the potentially lethal sprayer for days on end, keeping the generators kicking over day and night like frantic fiends from hell. Small plants died and birds fell from the air in the locality while residents complained of foul smells. Nevertheless, no humans died; it seems the method of transmission somehow failed to find a vector into the lucky residents of Tokyo.

Then in 1992, a well-funded team from the cult arrived in Zaire in Africa, now the Democratic Republic of Congo. Composed of at least 40 members, including the guru, they came with masses of cash and an avowed intention to help those struck down by the hemorrhagic fever Ebola. Their real mission was much more sinister, as they sought to obtain samples of the virus to further their diabolical schemes. The gruesome nature of this virulent disease was just what Asahara required for his doomsday scenario, though whether the group managed to safely transport any of the living virus back to Japan is unknown.

These were just some of the bizarre biological and chemical warfare schemes hatched by the cult. But while all of them ultimately failed, one experiment, the production of sarin, paid off with gruesome success.

A Deadly Plan

The main compound of the cult, situated below the picturesque heights of Mount Fuji, was divided into different buildings, all with a sinister part to play in Asahara's deadly schemes. At the heart of the compound was Satian 7, a nondescript three-story building. Near the entrance was a statue of Shiva, the Hindu god of destruction, an appropriate figure given that housed within the labyrinth of corridors and halls was a huge array of precursor chemicals for the production of nerve gas. Indeed, 10 million dollars was spent creating a state-of-the-art chemical processing plant with 100 staff, and high levels of security were employed, with armed guards ensuring only the most trusted members of the cult could gain access to the building's deadly secrets. Adding to these layers of security were sealed airproof bulkheads to prevent contamination, along with decontamination chambers to allow staff to get out of their pressurized biohazard suites. Satian 7 had one aim—to produce 17.6 lbs (8 kilos) of liquid sarin every day until 70 tonnes had been amassed. The scale of Asahara's bloodlust was immense; an average person can be killed by 6 milligrams of sarin absorbed by the skin and 551 lbs (250 kilos) could take out the entire population of central Washington.

The first sarin attack was a humiliating failure. In the early spring of 1994 a purpose-built sarin dispersal vehicle was dispatched to kill the leader of a rival religious organization. The cult members were all dressed in protective clothing and the truck had been equipped with a sarin dispersal system. But the difficult method of delivery was not yet foolproof and the truck caught fire. One member of the attack

team was exposed and the rest fled. Fortunately for the member he survived as, like all of the team, he had taken the sarin antidote before the raid.

ABOVE The police raid on Aum's facility, No. 7 Satyam, yielded deadly chemicals and weapons. Asahara was found hiding in a secret compartment.

If sarin is to be converted from a liquid form to a sprayable gas, it must first be heated above room temperature, an understandably hazardous procedure. After the fiasco of the first attack, a more sophisticated device was built and installed within a two-ton refrigerated truck. Three tanks of sarin, a computer-controlled heater, and a fan to disperse the lethal gas were included in the new, improved model, and on Monday June 27th the fully equipped death truck set off for Matsumoto, 60 miles from the cult headquarters. The initial target was a law court but due to unexpected delays the team arrived at the picturesque mountain town too late to spray their deadly cargo into the courthouse building. Asahara had decided to take out the Matsumoto law courts, and three presiding judges, to prevent a negative judgment in a land dispute. The three judges who were the target of the terrorist attack were staying in a small apartment block, so the van was positioned in a small square near the judges' accommodation.

The team of six halted the van, gave each other sarin antidote injections, donned their enviro-suits and fired up the dispersal unit. Soon the gas cloud was spewing into

ABOVE **The cult survives, despite the fact that its leadership is rotting on death row. Here, protestors demonstrate against its continued existence.**

the built-up area, forming a white cloud around the van before it dissipated and settled lower-down on the ground, where gentle breezes wafted it through the small township.

Investigators were later able to trace the course of the deadly gas. Trees, grasses, and shrubs as well as small animals or birds all died as soon as the lethal vapor touched them. The gas insinuated itself into the adjoining properties. Those who were asleep with their windows and doors closed were fortunate to escape with mild, almost flu-like symptoms. Others were not so lucky. The first symptoms varied, but a severe coughing fit was common, followed soon after by dimmed light or fractured eyesight, dizziness, an inability to breathe, and nausea. Those who felt the full effect then began writhing in pain as their body sent crazed electrical impulses into nerves and muscles, many thrashing around so violently that they bruised themselves severely while coughing up blood.

This was a particularly pure batch that killed 13 innocent civilians and wounded many more. They all required extensive hospitalization, and most suffered permanent damage to their senses and internal organs. Although the judges survived, one barely, the attack was declared a success.

The cult members emptied the sarin vats and made a clear getaway, leaving chaos and confusion behind them. Fortunately for the Aum Shinrikyo perpetrators, suspicion soon fell on an industrial chemist who lived in the area. He was immediately identified as the main suspect and almost paraded in the media, who understandably were baying for a scapegoat. The fact that he was storing some fairly harmless chemicals was what initially attracted suspicion. Unsurprisingly, the authorities could not find a motive or a means for the man they had apprehended, but so strong were their suspicions that they precluded intensive police investigation into the real cause.

After several months the chemist was cleared and the police got a heads-up as to the real culprits. Farmers near the main Aum compound had been complaining of noxious gases being emitted from the base. were dying and plants were withering, and chemical analysis of the surrounding soil revealed the unmistakable signature of sarin and its precursor chemicals.

Finally, after years of inaction the police decided to search the compound. The local police placed a request to borrow hazardous materials suits and gasmasks from the military. This led to two sergeants who were members of Aum hearing of the unusual request. They immediately alerted the cult leadership, tipping them off to the impending raid.

It was essential to stop the investigation. Various plots were hatched: a truck filled with TNT could be used to blow up police headquarters; the new, improved laser could cut the building in half; or mustard gas and cyanide could be sprayed over the headquarters by the Soviet-built Mi-17 attack chopper. For various reasons, none of these crazy options were chosen.

Shoko Asahara decided to move before the police. He would bring on Armageddon and cause such a scene of mayhem and murder that the authorities would be paralyzed. He ordered his most daring attack—mass murder on the Tokyo subway, one of the most extensive transport networks in the world, carrying 5 million people every day. Included in this massive payload were large numbers of Japanese police officers. At 8:30 a.m., the height of rush hour, one law enforcement shift comes on while the other goes off duty. The police tend to congregate in certain cars, and these would be the main target.

Tokyo Attack

On the morning of March 20, 1995, the five-man terrorist squad, most of them with university science degrees, left Satian 7 in the Aum compound and drove to Tokyo. Each was armed with a carryall containing two or three vacuum-sealed plastic bags each with a 30 percent solution of Sarin. Asahara had complained that the sarin used in the Matsumoto attacks had been too pure. This change to a weaker solution probably saved hundreds of thousands of lives. Each man was also equipped with an umbrella with a sharpened tip. They had practiced the previous evening gently puncturing bags so that the poison would leach out of the bag, gradually flowing out and moving into the environment.

Each man had had his target chosen by the planners during an earlier reconnaissance. Trains were favored carrying the most passengers, moving through the heart of Tokyo's Central Business District, as these would expose most commuters to the gas.

The attack was meticulously planned. Each of the killers was ferried to his designated subway station by a chauffeured car. As they approached their target they wrapped their deadly parcels in newspaper before descending underground. As the selected trains opened their doors they squeezed in and found a seat near to a door, placed their packages on the ground and, waiting for the designated station where they were due to picked up by their driver, held the umbrellas poised over the sarin bags. As the trains drew to a halt at the appointed station each of the cult members ruptured the plastic membranes

BELOW **A Tokyo fire department member evacuates a victim during an anti-terrorism drill. Scenes like this shocked the Japanese during the Sarin attacks of 1995.**

allowing the sarin to soak into the newspaper wrapping through the bags and onto the floor. It then began gently to evaporate into the environment. Even though they had taken antidote pills beforehand, the five exited the trains immediately, before proceeding up the escalators to rendezvous with their drivers for the journey back to the Aum Shinrikyo compound.

Those traveling in the subway were not so fortunate. As the sarin leaked out of the bags it formed dark dirty puddles near the doors of five trains, commuters walking through the noxious agent spreading it into other carriages and onto platforms throughout the underground system.

The first thing that many noticed was an acrid stench. Pure sarin is odorless, but this batch was filled with impurities. Some thought it smelt of mustard; others were reminded of burning rubber. Whatever the smell, the effects were the same, as whole carriages of people began to retch and heave. There was no respite, as the deadly gas had quickly penetrated deep into their lungs. The train drivers, not immediately realizing anything was amiss, closed the carriage doors and proceeded to the next

ABOVE A wanted poster for Aum cult members. Even as late as 2009, many of those who helped mastermind Aum's crimes were still on the run.

stop. The sarin became denser and passengers began to drop dead. Those with less exposure fled the cars, bolting for the platform and the stairs or escalators to the surface. But the side effects of the poison added to the confusion. Many lost their sight or were blinded by splitting headaches, and only after the pandemonium reached epic proportions did the transport officials realize something was dreadfully wrong. The loudspeakers, usually restricted to announcing arrivals and departures, bellowed out evacuation procedures, but it was more than many could do merely to reach the surface, and those who made it collapsed in their thousands, waiting for emergency assistance. The scale of the catastrophe overwhelmed emergency services. Some 5,500 innocent citizens were hospitalized, with many permanently blinded and disabled. Surprisingly only 12 people died. Had pure sarin been used, this figure would no doubt have been in the thousands.

In fact, the cult had enough raw materials to produce sarin that could kill four million people. Immediately after the attack, raids were carried out throughout Japan on Aum installations; 1,200 barrels of toxic chemicals were found, including cyanide and mustard gas. Hundreds of punishment cells were also discovered, where cultists were starved almost to death and held in total sensory deprivation. No bodies were found, but in the main compound 80 barrels covered in soot were recovered near the microwave building. Whether one, two, or more cult members' bodies had been disposed of in each of these barrels was never revealed.

Some members of the cult scattered to carry out a program of resistance which included further assassinations. Asahara himself seemed to vanish into thin air. Although a convoy including a limousine carrying a bearded fat man was seen traveling through the streets of Tokyo, he could not be tracked down.

It wasn't until May 16, 1995 that police armed with hacksaws, angle grinders, and blowtorches penetrated the depths of Satian 6, another building in Aum's compound, and hacked open a tiny chamber buried deep within the complex. Inside they found the guru equipped with medicine, a Kalashnikov, and 100,000 dollars in cash.

By 1996, 350 cult leaders were being tried for various crimes including mass murder, kidnapping, and extortion. Asahara himself was defended by 12 lawyers but on February 27, 2004 he was sentenced to death. Today he still sits on death row, along with 13 other members of his cult. The Japanese are notoriously reluctant to carry out death sentences. Small remnants of the cult still exist, mostly in Japan and Russia. They have by and large renounced the doomsday prophecies of Asahara, although they are still kept under tight surveillance by police.

BELOW An Aum member in Russia meditating in front of Shoko Asahara's portrait in order to connect with him telepathically.

SARIN GAS (O-ISOPROPYL methylphosphonofluoridate), also called GB, is one of the most dangerous and toxic chemicals known. It belongs to a class of chemical weapons known as nerve agents, all of which are organophosphates. The G nerve agents, including tabun, sarin, and soman, are all extremely toxic, but not very persistent in the environment.

Sarin was first synthesized as a pesticide in 1938 by a group of German scientists. The Nazi state produced at least 10 tons of the lethal toxin but Hitler's unwillingness to use chemical warfare on the battlefield meant it was not deployed, although many artillery shells were filled as a potential delivery mechanism. The Soviets later captured the manufacturing plant and produced at least 12,000 tons of their own. The Americans have approximately 5,000 tons stockpiled. None of these major powers have ever used it.

Middle Eastern rulers have not been so shy. Iraq under Saddam Hussein used nerve agents including sarin against Kurdish separatists, killing at least 5,000 innocent Kurds and wounding 65,000. In the ongoing Syrian conflict, forces loyal to President Assad have deployed the weapon against rebel areas, killing and injuring many civilians.

Nerve agents such as sarin cause their toxic effects by preventing the proper operation of an enzyme that acts as the body's "off switch" for glands and muscles, which otherwise would suffer constant stimulation. As reported in the subway gassings, symptoms of sarin poisoning range from mildly irritating to deadly. Some 500 times more deadly than cyanide, just 0.5 milligrams is considered a lethal dose

Initial symptoms of poisoning include a runny nose, watery eyes, and drooling or excessive sweating, caused by the drug sending the body's normal restorative functions into overdrive. These symptoms are followed by blurred or limited vision, hacking cough, chest tightening, confusion, weakness, and drowsiness. In those with greater exposure, the body's systems go into meltdown. Uncontrolled vomiting, urinating, and diarrhea lead the patients to soil themselves before their heart rate accelerates. The body then spasms and its respiratory and circulatory systems collapse.

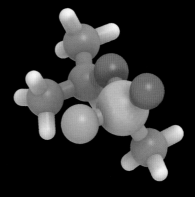

RIGHT The Sarin gas molecule. One tiny drop on the skin can be lethal. Heat turns it into a gaseous form, allowing the chemical to spread rapidly.

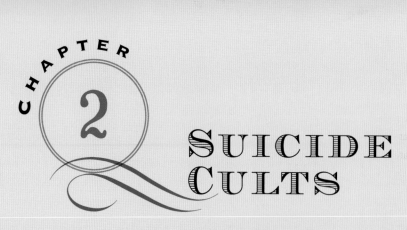

CHAPTER 2

SUICIDE CULTS

SUICIDE CULTS ARE PERHAPS THE SADDEST of all. Like most cults the leaders prey on weak or isolated individuals, tempting them with all manner of promises. But these cults are different. Once the members are ensnared in the bizarre psychological web of beliefs and practices, the leader's thoughts turn to death, though not of outsiders but of the cult members themselves through mass suicide. In some cases, the members commit suicide gladly; in others, the unwilling are killed by force.

THE SUMERIANS

The first known evidence of a suicide cult was found in the burial pits of Sumerian kings. The early kings and queens of the city of Ur were not buried alone. In fact, the earliest graves were dated to around 3500 BCE and show that the Sumerians were inheritors of a belief system that entailed burying not just tools, food, weapons, and clothes to assist the deceased in the afterlife, but human help, too.

The Great Death Pit, discovered by Leonard Woolley during his 1922–1934 excavations, contained 74 attendants who had been killed to accompany the ruler in his afterlife. This nameless king obviously had a taste for the ladies, as 68 of the 74 were young women. They were neatly arranged in four rows and dressed in luxurious scarlet robes, with elaborate coiffures decorated with an abundance of bejewelled silver and gold headdresses. The women appeared to be privileged and had cups or shells containing cosmetics and jars containing foodstuffs. Their master obviously wanted his harem to look good in the afterlife and supply him with plenty of food. Six women were equipped with lyres and harps, no doubt intended to provide the heavenly entertainment. One woman was found gripping her headdress and Woolley concluded that she had been in too much of a hurry, or too excited, to put it on.

Guarding this bevy of beauties were six fully armed soldiers equipped with helmets, spears, knives, and chariots. One chamber arrayed behind the soldiers had two fully equipped chariots complete with the beasts who pulled them in life.

Woolley presumed that all of the people he had found had been standing calmly in their designated location within the tombs

BELOW The Sumerian Standard of Ur. Soldiers and chariots similar to the ones depicted here were buried alongside the king in large burial chambers.

before they had been given a deathly potion which they willingly gulped down; as the poison took effect they calmly lay down and went to join their sovereign in the afterlife. However, modern reconstructive techniques paint an entirely different picture, finding that most were killed with a blow to the head by a mace or a thrust from a spear into the victim's brain. Some exhibit classic defensive wounds on the wrist and hand bones. Others were killed well before the burial and baked to preserve their corpses for the ceremony!

The Plant of Joy

If most of the Sumerian courtiers did go to their deaths peacefully it is likely that the potion that they drank would have included a large dose of opium. The first reference to the use of opium can be found in Sumerian texts dating back to 3300 BCE, where the sticky substance taken from the opium poppy *Papaver somniferum* is referred to as "hul-gil," or "the plant of joy." The potion may also have included beer, as the Sumerians used up to 40 percent of their barley output to produce this alcoholic beverage.

The Sumerians had a rich religious belief system and in all likelihood the juice of the opium poppy of was utilized as a means of entering the spiritual realm of the gods and communicating with unseen forces. Maybe the consumption was seen as a type of sacrifice to certain deities, guaranteeing abundant harvests and good luck.

Cups were found in some of the deposits and it is thought that opium was used as a sedative and possibly as part, if not all, of the poisoning agent. With their long history of using opium it is possible that the Sumerians had some means of concentrating the active ingredients leading to a potentially lethal brew if taken in a large enough dose. While this is speculation, it is likely that the sacrificial victims used the juice of the poppy to help usher them into a new existence.

THE FIRST REFERENCE TO THE USE OF OPIUM CAN BE FOUND IN SUMERIAN TEXTS DATING BACK TO 3300 BCE, WHERE THE STICKY SUBSTANCE TAKEN FROM THE OPIUM POPPY *PAPAVER SOMNIFERUM* IS REFERRED TO AS "HUL-GIL," OR "THE PLANT OF JOY."

Samurai Suicide

THE JAPANESE MYSTICAL ETHOS OF Bushido placed honor before all other considerations. Life was as "light as a feather," and its passing should have as much consequence as a leaf falling in autumn. With such a worldview it is no surprise that the samurai developed elaborate methods of committing suicide.

One of the key moments of a samurai's life was his death. A good death was necessary if he was to be remembered with respect and affection by later generations. *Seppuku* (stomach-slitting) was a form of ritualized suicide. There were four reasons why a samurai could commit seppuku: to avoid capture after battle; as a result of a death sentence handed down by a lord; as a protest against a superior's actions; or to follow one's lord into death, the ultimate sign of loyalty.

All samurai knew what was expected when carrying out the rite, and part of every father's responsibility was to teach his son how to perform the ritual. Each man had a short sword called the wakizashi. The doomed man would sit with crossed legs and holding the wakizashi in both hands plunge the blade into his intestines below his belly on the left side. This is no easy task as the stomach and guts are lined with tough sinewy lining. The samurai would then drag the blade across and below the belly to the right side, slicing through the stomach muscles before giving the blade a quick turn and an upward thrust toward the rib cage. So that it could be reported that he had had a good death, no expression of pain or gasp of agony could escape the warrior's lips.

Adding to the bizarre ritualization of the stomach slitting, which had been common since the 11th century, was the final act. A specially appointed kaishakunin (second) stood behind the condemned man with his sword upraised. Once suitable bravery had been displayed and the requisite cuts made, the kaishakunin brought his sword down in a swift act of decapitation. The second also had the responsibility of reporting that he had witnessed an "honorable" death.

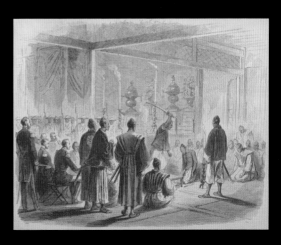

RIGHT **Once a Samurai had ripped open his innards with a short sword or dagger, his second finished the ritual by decapitating him with one blow.**

JIM JONES AND THE PEOPLES TEMPLE

Visitors who make a pilgrimage to the site of the Peoples Temple compound 150 miles (240 kilometers) west of the Guyanese capital of Georgetown are struck by its isolation. The 3,800-acre (1,537-hectare) site leased by Jim Jones in 1974 is far removed from any major towns, and the nearest watercourse is seven miles (11 kilometers) away.

There are few signs that it was once a large settlement. Jungle has reclaimed most of the terrain, and only a few relics remain. An old tractor, a rusted cassava mill, a filing cabinet, and a decrepit generator are pretty much all a recent expedition uncovered after searching for several hours. One more object was found—an old oil drum cut in half, with traces of white paint still adhering to its rusty surface.

The few remains make it almost impossible to imagine the dreadful scene enacted on November 18, 1978 when Jim Jones proclaimed the virtues of "revolutionary suicide" over the camp's loudspeaker while his followers swallowed a lethal concoction of poison and Kool-Aid. Where the occasional bird now calls to its mate, children screamed as they were injected with deadly needles filled with cyanide, while others sought to break through a cordon of armed guards to escape. They were to be hunted down and killed with forcibly administered cups of the

BELOW Not much remains of Jonestown in the jungles of Guyana. Jim Jones's idea of revolutionary suicide failed to change the world.

deadly draft. In all, 909 Americans died that day—not in rapture at being taken up to heaven but in the most horrific way imaginable, as cyanide coursed through their bodies and shut down their nervous systems.

The man responsible for so much death was born on May 13, 1931 in Crete, Indiana. His father was an ex-soldier who had been slightly unhinged by his experiences at the front in World War One, while his mother, Lynette, thought from an early age that she was going to give birth to the Messiah.

While most American children in the 1930s and '40s enjoyed playing "Cowboys and Injuns" or "Doctors and Nurses," the young Jim Jones had another game to play. He liked to imagine himself as a preacher and his friends were cast in the role of a rapt congregation. They would be damned to hell, healed with a holy touch, or praised to the lord. In the barn behind his house Jones would dress up with a biblical white robe over his shoulder and if no classmates were available he'd heal the family's flock of chickens. A precocious child, he read widely with a particular interest in the

Cyanide

Consumption of cyanide basically prevents blood from transferring oxygen to the cells. This has several nasty side effects including violent convulsions as muscles contract due to cell suffocation. One sure symptom of cyanide consumption is small bruises breaking out all over the body as the blood becomes saturated with oxygen. Even a small dose creates many unpleasant symptoms, including a general feeling of weakness and malaise. But the cult members of the

Peoples Temple were not given small doses; they were given lethal doses which immediately caused crippling abdominal pain, nausea, vomiting, and chest pain. Then they dropped unconscious to the ground, dying from respiratory collapse and cardiac arrest.

RIGHT **Cyanide is a harmless looking powder, but it is extremely lethal. Many high-ranking Nazis in World War Two used it to commit suicide on being captured.**

ABOVE **Jim Jones in San Francisco. He wore his sunglasses day and night, adding to his mystique. They also covered his increasingly drug-addled eyes.**

great dictators. Other kids saw him as weird and preoccupied with death while being similarly obsessed with religion. He did, in his formative years, develop a sympathy for the plight of African Americans, and as a young preacher genuinely sought to help this oppressed community. Indeed, many of those who accompanied Jones to Guyana were black, lured by his sympathetic message. They paid for their trust with their lives.

There may well have been a genuine kernel of social justice in the young Jim Jones's soul. Seeing poverty and racism all around him, he became involved in communist organizations. Aware that communists were being openly attacked in American society, he decided that the best way to spread socialism would be to join a church. He experimented with several institutions including Somerset Southside Methodist Church and the Seventh Day Baptist Church. He was enamored by the faith healing practiced by charismatic preachers and decided that this would be the way he would build his own following.

In 1955, he founded the Wings of Deliverance Church but it soon became known colloquially as the Peoples Temple. Based in Indiana, the church actively argued for desegregation of black and white and attracted a large African American congregation.

At the same time as he was proselytizing equal rights for all Americans, another darker strain began to emerge in Jones's worldview. During the 1950s the Cold War between America and the USSR had escalated, and by 1961 Jones was so convinced the world was on the brink of nuclear war that he shifted his family to Brazil. This developing paranoia was fueled by his increasing use of alcohol and drugs, a habit fed by the quantities of Quaaludes, valium, dexies (Dextroamphetamine), and cocaine his aids tracked down.

With its charismatic preacher now resident in another country, the Peoples Temple began to wane, so Jones decided to move back to America, ending up in California, where the cult again began to grow. But while Jones proclaimed himself a holy man, there was nothing holy in the tricks he used to con people into joining his flock. He was the ultimate snake-oil salesman, and his dedicated followers would stoop to any low to gull trusting members of the public.

By the 1970s Jones had his shtick down to a fine art. With his thick mane of dark hair and the sunglasses he wore at all times of day and night, the well-dressed "priest" was able to use his charismatic and fiery sermons to attract an ever-growing flock. Whether they were struck by poverty, racism, or loneliness, Jones was able to offer his new disciples what they needed. People searching for meaning and structure in their lives are classified as "seekers" by cult analysts, and Jones reaped a rich harvest of these lost souls.

Jones declared himself to be a true faith healer, claiming the titles of God, Jesus, Father, and Dad as it suited him. He supposedly became adept at the practice of clairvoyance, as well as faith healing, building a reputation that attracted hundreds to his sermons at the Peoples Temple. Jones or his staff would mingle with the audience picking up snippets of information: who had problems with a crop, whose sight was fading, which family was dealing with a recent death, and so on. Utilizing this information from the stage, he convinced an amazed audience that they were witnessing a true clairvoyant at work. Soon the hoaxes became more elaborate. His adherents would go through the garbage of potential marks or even call and pretend to be doing a Gallup poll to find out useful information. Any information would be passed to Jones who would read small strips of paper surreptitiously as he called out an individual's life story. The ever-present sunglasses prevented the audience seeing what he was up to.

Being a fine illusionist, Jones was able to convince many witnesses of his healing abilities. A dedicated hardcore of believers would dress up as invalids, even going as far as having plaster placed over a supposedly broken limb. Jones would then miraculously "heal" the poor patient, who with much fanfare would throw off the plaster or get out of a wheelchair (though diligent investigative journalists noticed that those being healed in the afternoon session looked remarkably like those being healed in the evening show). Little frail-limbed old ladies who came to the Temple were offered vitamins, which in reality were drinks laced with sedatives that would knock the old women out. When they came to, the elderly women found themselves on stage with a cast on their leg and an explanation that the limb had been broken during the fainting fit. To the amazement of the rest of the audience Jones would then "heal" the old woman's leg and take off the cast. It is doubtful that many, given the euphoria of the moment and the adulation of the crowd, would kick up too much of a fuss or try to call Jones out on his fraud. Even more dramatically, drugs were used to make some of his flock "drop dead." A cult medical team would announce that all life signs had ceased, then, just as the drug began to wear off, Jones would approach the "corpse" and revive him with his "touch of God."

BELOW Jim Jones and his wife, Marceline Jones, pose with some of their adopted children. Scenes like this became rarer as Jones became obsessed with suicide.

In 1972 Jones resurrected himself! While mingling with parishioners in front of the Redwood Valley Mission, he screamed and fell to the ground, blood pouring from what seemed to be a bullet wound in his chest. The seemingly mortally wounded Jones was hustled into the parsonage but miraculously emerged, fully healed, soon after.

During the early seventies Jones was at the peak of his powers. People flocked to see the fantastically energetic sermons, and the Peoples Temple grew throughout California, with all major urban centers having a chapter. Jones was able to use his influence to swing elections in favor of his chosen candidates, and this power was traded for many favors.

It was around this time that another trait began to emerge in Jones's ever more disturbing behavior: not only was he becoming increasingly megalomaniac and paranoid, but he became unable to let cult members leave his clutches. Now they were encouraged to give up all their worldly goods to the church, while weaker individuals were badgered until they moved into crowded cult dorms, where they lived in squalid conditions with few of the comforts of modern life. Sex was frowned on and families were split up. Children were farmed out to foster parents or into communes while their parents were separated physically and emotionally. (As usual with messianic cult leaders, being exempt from such strictures, Jones himself had sex with many female congregation members.) But this was nothing compared to what happened to those who sought to leave the cult or even criticized it.

Jones's key weapon against any "rebels" was the force of his personality. He didn't hesitate to berate members of his flock who broke the increasingly stringent rules. By the time the cult had relocated to Guyana, these public humiliations had turned into mass hate sessions where the entire congregation of 900 people would scream and hurl abuse at the unfortunate victims. When members joined the cult, they were not only asked to hand over all their assets but also required to sign statutory declarations which were routinely left blank. These "attendances" or "meditations," as they were called, were Jones's insurance policies—should any member of the flock earn his ire, he could write false confessions in which the member appeared to own up to crimes such as theft, pedophilia, or rape. Clauses granting the cult power of attorney, as well as last wills and testaments, could be typed onto the documents, which were then handed to cult lawyers who would use them to strip parents of custody of their children.

Members were asked to prove their loyalty by writing statements explaining that they would kill anybody who sought to injure the movement.

Increasingly, meetings degenerated into violence. Initially, during the 1960s and early '70s, parishioners received a gentle rebuke by way of criticism. Other members would suggest means by which the individual could improve their behavior or attitude. But these attacks became more virulent over the years until at one meeting, in the heart of Middle America, Jones commanded that a member be spanked with a belt. Soon whole groups were being physically disciplined for minor transgressions such as smoking or drinking.

In 1972 a flat plank of wood was introduced—known as the "Board of Education"—with which children were beaten senseless in front of the congregation. Parents could not come to the rescue of their offspring, as this would invite punishments and accusations of disloyalty. Other children were locked in dark closets and given electric shocks after being berated over the PA. Jones used the microphone as a weapon against his flock. After punishment the transgressor, beaten and by now humiliated, had to say "Thank you, Father" into the microphone.

If a member sought to leave, they would be harassed by phone calls and with threatening letters. By 1975 Jones had decided no one was allowed to leave, so those who were brave enough to earn his disfavor and flee were well advised to relocate to the East Coast, thousands of miles away. That way they were less likely to receive visits in the middle of the night in which Jones's aides would leave threatening letters, or get late-night abusive phone calls. Even more intimidating, hearses were hired and left to idle outside defectors' houses or else fake obituaries were placed in local papers, and as a last resort Jones would send his aides to seize fleeing members.

Nevertheless, a steady stream of cult members managed to leave. Most were content to be left alone; after all, Jones had their "attendances" and "meditations" to hold over their heads as a Damoclean threat. Some did go to the press and some of the mud began to stick as accusations of violence, brainwashing, and theft were leveled against the Peoples Temple.

The Move to Jonestown

Jones decided he needed to escape any supervision by the American authorities and in October 1973 "The Commission," Jones's inner circle, decided to obtain land in Guyana and establish an agricultural commune they would run along socialist lines. It was to be called, of course, Jonestown.

In 1974 the first pioneers arrived at the unpromising tract of forest and began clearing it. The land itself was scrubby rainforest and was not suitable for intensive agriculture. The locals used slash-and-burn-type farming, which involved cutting down sections of forest and burning it to allow nutrients from the ash to enter the soil. This richer soil would be good for one or two harvests before the nutrients were leached out by crops and rain. It was in this isolated, hostile environment that the cult put down its roots.

The colonists sent glowing letters home talking of the balmy weather and the abundant crops they were growing. These letters were read out to Jones's congregations

and showed the huge potential of the promised land. According to these early communications the water was purer than glacial melt and all would live in harmony, free from interference from the government. A socialist utopia would be built.

ABOVE The entrance to Jonestown in Guyana. The promised socialist paradise soon turned into hell on earth. Once you passed these gates there was no return.

Like all things associated with the Peoples Temple there was not a lot of truth in these missives. The jungle was like a relentless foe. One area would be cleared by the colonists and their Amerindian employees only to grow back almost overnight. Experimental crops soon died from insect infestations or rust brought about by the humid weather. Chickens died and even pigs would only flourish for a short time before wasting away.

But the colonists persisted. A slow trickle of machinery arrived at the colony and gradually, over two or three years, housing was built and crops began to be harvested. Despite the hardships the first settlers even enjoyed their time, there being a genuine feeling that they were working for a brighter future.

But when Jones arrived in Guyana in 1977 to avoid increasing scrutiny from the press, the mood darkened in the "socialist utopia." They were now forbidden from watching movies; instead Soviet propaganda was shown, or dire news forecasts with lengthy diatribes from Jones reflecting his increasingly paranoid worldview.

The only communication out of Jonestown was by shortwave radio and infrequent mail. Like all good cult leaders Jones ensured that he alone had control of information. The only letters read by cultists back in the States were packed with uniformly good news. In addition, Jones produced propaganda movies of the good life being had by all. Meals of unlimited quantities of fried chicken, comfortable dorms, smiling faces, and well-staffed schools were filmed with a benevolent and fatherly Jones describing the wonderful life the members were living.

There was a reason for this. Jones wanted to get all of his congregation to migrate to Jonestown. In his own mind he was becoming increasingly fixated on the idea of mass suicide.

BELOW Jones used propaganda to lure his parishioners to Jonestown. But when they arrived, the parishioners found crowded, rat-infested accommodation.

Members were encouraged to move from the USA by a variety of typically underhand methods. A cadre of hardcore cultists would descend on a church dorm first thing in the morning and tell the selected members to pack as Jones wanted them immediately. Each member of the cadres had their own role to play. Some would

hustle the disorientated members while the others acted sympathetic and reassuring. Veiled threats were used. Food would be refused and family members would abandon any who did not follow Jones's summons. Others guarded the phones to prevent calls being made to outsiders. If any began to resist, a group of "troubleshooters" descended on them and used any means possible to get them into the waiting buses. Various false reassurances were given: you can return after a week or so if you are not happy; we'll bring your pet along afterward, and so on.

In order to conceal the exodus, the new colonists were taken out in dribs and drabs, using different airports. Jones was desperate to avoid any further controversy.

Once they arrived at Jonestown only the most devoted of Jones's followers could not have been disappointed. Eventually, some 900 people were packed into 50 or so ramshackle huts crammed with bunk beds. None had refrigeration or food storage or even fans to help cool the stifling jungle humidity. Showing his true colors, Jones had become a fanatical communist. He imposed upon his followers the North Korean invention of eight hours working and eight hours learning each day. The work was unpleasant. While harassed by thousands of biting insects, the parishioners were required to lug buckets of water from a creek to irrigate the struggling crops. Others did maintenance to clear rust from machinery, while all clothes and bedding were constantly under attack from mildew and mold. On arrival they had handed over any cash and their passports for "safekeeping." They were trapped.

Meals were a disappointment. Rather than the sumptuous food shown on the propaganda pictures, all were awoken at 7:00 a.m. to have a cold shower (there was no heated water) before attending the central pavilion where a watery porridge with maybe a bit of fresh fruit was served up. After working all day, a small meal would be served, mainly composed of local starches or some rice and maybe a small vegetable. The leader, of course, had an air-conditioned hut with a fridge stacked with ice lollies, alcohol, and decent food. Jones had a near mutiny on his hands when a promised pork meal—two pigs were going to be slaughtered—turned out to include only a tiny morsel for each individual in a watery stew. Diarrhea became endemic. Even on the one occasion when Jones opened the purse strings and supplied a chicken dinner for them, rather than letting them enjoy the treat Jones berated his followers over the PA system for their selfishness.

This was the other feature that turned Jonestown into a living hell. With a captive audience he could unleash his venomous sermonizing on them 24/7. After working all day, the flock were summoned to the central pavilion where Jones delivered his latest diatribe against whatever issue appealed to him as an appropriate target for his venom. Whether it was the Christian Bible, the American government, or individuals within the cult, he would hurl abuse and sermonize for hours. Jones rose at midday, so it was no problem for him to ramble on all night. But any who fell asleep during

ABOVE Jones outside with cult members in Jonestown. The smiling faces belie the bullying and intimidation that were used to keep members in line.

these interminable ravings were rudely woken up, and none except the ill were able to stay in their cabins to avoid the verbal onslaught.

The "socialist utopia" began to resemble a prison camp. There were always guards armed with rifles, crossbows, and clubs, ostensibly to protect the flock from outside interference but really to keep the residents in line. Small misdemeanors such as smoking were punished with a cane. Other law breakers were stuck in a small wooden box or chained to a log if the "crimes" were more serious. Any who tried to flee would be humiliated and verbally attacked by the entire 900-strong congregation, and would have their head shaved as a mark of shame. Elderly residents unable to deal with the pressure and temperature were knocked out with drugs and confined to the hospital or to their quarters.

The fate that all members dreaded the most was to be put on the "learning crew." Those who spoke out against the conditions were forced to live in a particularly crowded dorm without enough bedding. They were not allowed to communicate with anybody, and toiled all day at the most degrading and dangerous tasks. They were forced to run from point to point and were deemed to be third-class citizens.

As early as 1973 Jones had the notion of attracting attention to the cult by getting members to commit suicide. Over the years he refined this idea into the concept of "revolutionary suicide." He fantasized about mass suicide and even referred during some sermons to dying with 900 other people as being the ultimate orgasm.

Once the flock was confined in Jonestown this became more and more of an obsession. When he first mentioned it, only a small number of his followers voted for suicide, but as he continued to espouse its virtues more and more came over to his way of thinking. Regular votes were held on the topic and any who didn't vote for it were placed on lists and received fewer rations or copped abuse from Jones's closest followers. The votes became more and more common. Those who did not vote for suicide were taken by armed guards to the podium where Jones would harangue and abuse them until they changed their minds. Many voted to commit suicide so they could get some sleep. Once the leader felt he had convinced all of his flock, he would let them return to their cramped quarters and get a few hours' sleep before the new day began.

As Jones became more paranoid, his rantings over the camp PA became more and more strident. The American government, the FBI, the army, and the air force were all seen as potential threats. But even though his drug-fueled fantasies of revolutionary suicide became more vivid, he still had an understanding that it was necessary to make his followers adjust to the need for annihilation. His warm-ups were called White Nights.

By this time Jonestown was beginning to resemble an armed camp. There were upward of 40 weapons at the guards' disposal, including Ruger telescopic rifles, as well as Remingtons, shotguns, and .38 semi-automatic pistols. Whenever Jones lectured them over the PA the residents of Jonestown were forbidden to talk and could be beaten if they broke this rule. Even when he was not there, tape recordings of his thoughts could be broadcast 24/7. But in dramatic interventions, the interminable dirge would be interrupted quite suddenly, as Jones, taking everybody by surprise, yelled out "White Night! White Night!! We are all in danger. The American government is putting all of the negroes in concentration camps and they are coming to get us." He would exhort everybody to run to the central pavilion where he would build up into a paroxysm of hysterical panic. "We are building a socialist utopia. We threaten the very basis of the USA's government. They are coming to arrest and torture you all. We cannot let it happen." At the same time his trusted lieutenants would open up with automatic gunfire from the fringes of the jungle, all the while letting out warlike shrieks. Others would pretend to run in an effort to escape, only to be shot by rubber bullets and hit the dirt screaming.

The medical teams then poured out of the medical center armed with large tubs of Kool-Aid and mounds of paper cups. "Drink the medicine, they will not take us alive," Jones shrieked, and often in the panic of the moment most would. Surrounding the parishioners were other armed guards, making sure all drank the Kool-Aid and threatening to shoot if the order was not carried out. Of those who downed the draft, some dropped to the ground vomiting or fainting, convinced psychologically that they were about to die, while others just sat and wondered why they still survived.

When all had done as they were told, Jones's voice broke into uproarious laughter. "Now I can trust you," he said. "Don't worry, this was just a rehearsal. Go to bed and get a good night's rest."

At other times the whole population were turned out of bed, issued rudimentary weapons such as knives and hoes and forced to stand guard all night until dawn saw them dropping from exhaustion.

Gradually, the White Nights did the trick, so that when there was in fact a real crisis, most of his flock was conditioned to accept suicide as a possible and even likely outcome. Indeed, by now Jones and his inner cohort were planning for the final event. In what was dubbed the "last stand plan," his closest lieutenants swore to follow him in suicide. Each had their allotted role in the coming Armageddon. "Angels" were appointed to survive the suicide. It was their role to hunt down and kill any defectors and public officials who had offended their leader. The poison had been sourced, the medical team prepared, and most of the cult's members psychologically primed for mass suicide. All that was needed was a crisis.

A Troubled Leader

By late 1978 the pressure was starting to build on Jones. Several ex-cult members were suing for the return of their children, giving further bad publicity to Jones's activities. The cases were a litmus test. If Jones lost custody, all of his followers would see him as a mere human being.

One of the few things keeping Jonestown afloat was the inhabitants' social security payments which went straight into Jones's accounts. Then the government placed a halt order on all further payments. Moreover, US Customs were now taking a close look at materials sent to Guyana, fueling Jones's mounting paranoia. Even his government contacts in the undeveloped nation were less willing to extend him favors.

These calamities were exacerbated when some members escaped and complained to the local police that they were being treated like slaves. An organization called the Concerned Relatives was enlisting aid from all sectors of government, and it

was clear that although Jones had fled America, the US authorities were not going to leave the Peoples Temple to its own devices. More and more reports were being made discussing Jones's obsession with suicide. This heightened fears among relatives left behind.

But the critical tinder for the coming tragedy was Jones's increasing drug use and, ultimately, the death of his mother. The loss of this one last link with reality seemed to send him over the edge into madness. Reports from survivors say he was losing control of his bodily functions. He wore sunglasses around the clock so as to conceal his bloodshot eyes and haggard appearance. His tongue seemed to be loose and flaccid, and Jones often mispronounced words as his rambling became slurred and difficult to understand. He spent entire days and nights locked up in his cabin where his paranoid delusions became worse and worse. Rather than blaming the drugs he developed many conspiracy theories for his deteriorating mental condition—one being that the Guyanese were poisoning the wells, and another that the US government was flying crop dusters at night, spraying Jonestown with poisons and hallucinogenics. Nevertheless, despite his sorry state he retained the loyalty of his closest confidants and continued to be serviced by several girlfriends, while armed guards surrounded his hut and supervised the meals being prepared for him, alert to any attempts at poisoning. Jones himself carried a Magnum .357 in his waistband and prepared for the last White Night.

BELOW A Kool-Aid packet. This sweet fizzy drink was used to conceal the bitter taste of the sedative chloral hydrate and the poison potassium cyanide.

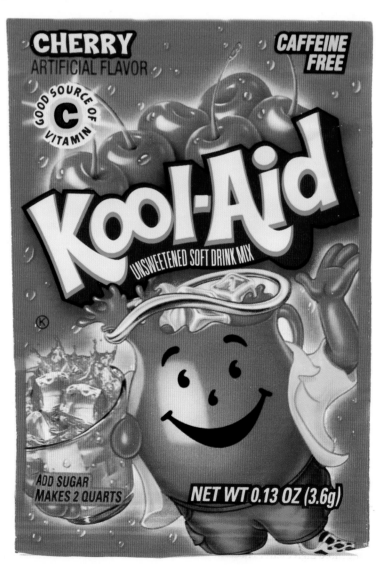

A Lethal Dose

Jones's pet doctor (trained but not registered), charged with maintaining Jones's supply of recreational uppers and downers, was one Laurence Eugene Schacht (1948–78). It was Schacht who worked out it would take 250 mg of cyanide to kill a single adult, and he who purchased $8.85 worth of sodium cyanide, just one pound (454 g), which was more than enough to kill 900 innocent people.

He also investigated other means to kill his boss's flock. In fact, Schacht was the only doctor for the entire encampment of 1,000 people and as such was run ragged by a range of tropical complaints and rashes, only managing to get to sleep at night by knocking himself out with Valium. Fortunately, Jones recognized the doctor's worth and gave him a day off every Wednesday.

Rather than rest, with a missionary zeal that no doubt delighted his master Schacht used these free days to experiment with different lethal concoctions, including tetanus, botulism, and staphylococcus. Just like Shoko Asahara, Schacht saw a lot of promise in botulism as a weapon of mass slaughter. Several outbreaks of food poisoning had killed many people back in the US, and he knew that only a tiny amount was required for a lethal dose. The shortcomings of this pathogen were its slow incubation process and the fact that once symptoms arose such as difficulty swallowing and slurred speech, it could still take up to three days for the patient to die.

Like an archetypal mad scientist Schacht toiled away in his primitive lab stuck in the middle of a tropical jungle, with heat beating down on the building's tin roof, testing new cultures and desperately trying to come up with a lethal method to achieve Jones's crazy goal of mass suicide. But while his experiments had an unsurprisingly low success rate, Schacht and the camp's head nurse, Phyllis Chaikin (1939–78), did at least develop a protocol for mass slaughter.

Guards at the Nazi extermination camps of Operation Reinhard would have appreciated the meticulous procedures and timings worked out by doctor and nurse. Syringes were procured and a timetable worked out, determining which of his medical support team would "graduate" which members of the colony. This included the need to separate mothers from infants and the creation of work stations so that the maximum number of individuals could be killed in the shortest possible time. Schacht decided that he and Parks would kill the medical teams once they had done their work, and finally the two would "graduate" each other.

These procedures were practiced on White Nights as Jones whipped up his flock into a paranoid fervor to see exactly who would follow his commands to commit revolutionary suicide. These dress rehearsals for mass death revealed a flaw—the parishioners were reluctant to swallow foul-tasting concoctions—so Schacht ordered one more ingredient to help the medicine go down: orange Kool-Aid.

ABOVE Congressman Leo Ryan responded to the pleas of desperate family members concerned about their relatives in Jonestown. He paid for his concern with his life.

By this point, Schacht's mental state was also deteriorating. He had amassed so many lethal drugs that he needed a constant supply of sedatives to deal with the enormity of the crime he was about to commit. He became a lonely figure as he walked around Jonestown, talking to himself while subject to uncontrollable fits of shaking.

Under Scrutiny

Congressman Leo Ryan (1925–78) decided Jonestown needed to be investigated. The son of a friend had died in mysterious circumstances and the crusading Democratic politician was determined to find out if the rumors of violence and intimidation at the settlement were true. He assembled a team that included print and television journalists and members of the Concerned Relatives committee. On Wednesday November 15th he arrived in Guyana and on the 17th he boarded a chartered plane and the party flew to the airstrip at Port Kaituma, a 20-minute drive from the settlement. Jones had done everything in his power to stop the party getting that far. His Guyanese allies tried to arrest some of the party on trumped-up currency violations and threatened to cancel the visas. Reservations in the local hotels were canceled, and once they had boarded the plane to the cult compound a false report was radioed to air traffic control saying the airstrip was too wet for a safe landing. Even after the Congressmen's party had landed and was making its way to Jonestown, its route was obstructed by roadblocks of fallen logs, which took several hours to clear.

It wasn't until five o'clock in the afternoon that the party, which included four relatives of cult members and eight journalists, finally reached Jonestown. One of Jones's closest aides tried to do a snow job on Ryan, but he insisted on talking to Jones. Half an hour later Jones arrived. Flanked by his lawyers he was wearing a bright red shirt and his trademark sunglasses. Ryan was not to know that the previous night Jones had held a rally whipping up hate against the congressman.

Initially, the meeting went well. Jones seemed to be acting reasonably and as journalists fanned out into the encampment most of the residents appeared satisfied with their lot. Some family members were present among the party and sought to convince their relatives to leave with them. All were insistent on staying.

Journalists kept a filmed record of what went on in Jonestown that day and this footage, as well as the taped recording of Jones as soon afterward he exhorts his flock to "revolutionary suicide," is readily available, a unique record of a mass tragedy. The footage of Guyanese authorities and Americans visiting the site soon after the massacre is also available.

As the journalists, many of whom would soon be dead, filmed the residents, tension seemed to build. Watching the footage, you sense that behind the assurances that they are content with their lives, there is a quiet desperation. All the responses are remarkably similar, hinting at the training they had been given in preparation for this visit. You get the feeling that Jones's enforcers are hanging about just out of camera shot, making sure that only the correct responses are given. The delegation was not to know who these enforcers were; they were all dressed the same as the rest of the flock. But when the cameras weren't there the residents knew exactly who held the weapons and clubs that ensured all were kept in line. The smiles are reminiscent

AS THE JOURNALISTS, MANY OF WHOM WOULD SOON BE DEAD, FILMED THE RESIDENTS, TENSION SEEMED TO BUILD. WATCHING THE FOOTAGE, YOU SENSE THAT BEHIND THE ASSURANCES THAT THEY ARE CONTENT WITH THEIR LIVES, THERE IS A QUIET DESPERATION.

ABOVE Members of the news team who traveled with Congressman Ryan to Guyana. Many would be gunned down soon after this photo was taken.

of the Chinese filmed during the Great Leap Forward in the late 1950s. Ordered to smile at all costs, many adopted a rictus grin even though their faces were obviously hurting.

Nonetheless, the picture of a happy community seemed to be holding up well and when Congressman Ryan addressed all the residents in the pavilion later in the evening and said he was tremendously impressed with everything he saw, everybody erupted into a storm of frenzied applause that seemed to last forever and almost brought the tin roof crashing down.

But, as the television news footage makes clear, the applause is way too much. Ryan looks uncomfortable as it goes on for so long and has a frenetic, almost hysterical enthusiasm. Perhaps his words of praise allowed the members to contemplate that with government approval White Nights would no longer be necessary and the future maybe looked bright after all.

All the same, the next day the wheels fell off the elaborate charade. Members of the Peoples Temple approached some of the delegates and surreptitiously handed over hastily scrawled notes. They wanted to get out. A small trickle soon became a flood and up to 30 individuals began to grab their meager possessions and make their way toward the large Mack truck that was about to return to the airport. While they all appeared impassive the tension in the air was thick as they desperately waited for the truck to leave.

Groups approached Jones pleading their case. They still loved him, the men and women declared, they saw what he was doing as fantastic, but they had to leave. Jones was not happy but managed to contain his rage, talking reasonably as he approached each individual and almost begging them to stay.

But it was all to no avail, as the truck filled up with the desperate evacuees, and a last shot of Jones showed his true colors. He was seen surrounded by cronies coming up with a plan, his eyes furious behind his dark glasses.

Then, next thing, one of the cult leader's most trusted men detached himself from the group and joined the fleeing residents, who immediately became distressed, as they knew he was up to no good. His role was to shoot the pilot of the escape plane with the senator, ensuring that all died in a blazing fireball in the Uruguay jungle.

Ryan had chosen to remain another night at Jonestown, but one of Jones's supporters suddenly attacked him with a knife, and the Congressman, although unharmed, decided to leave with the waiting truck. The relief of all must have been tremendous as the truck emerged from the claustrophobic jungle lane and approached the landing strip.

Jones was not going to let anyone escape. Before they had boarded the plane, a tray truck had reached the makeshift runway and disgorged some of the camp's toughest enforcers. Well armed with rifles and shotguns, they gunned down journalists, officials, and cult members alike. Ryan tried to find shelter behind one of the plane's wheels but died from multiple gunshots.

A Revolutionary Suicide

Jones had the crisis he wanted. He was about to execute the long-anticipated plan of revolutionary suicide. The residents of Jonestown were summoned to the pavilion. One can only imagine their feelings. They had experienced a rollercoaster of emotions in the previous few days. Hope and fear must have played merry havoc with their minds. They were vulnerable and confused, just the way Jones wanted them. As they sat in the pavilion, many noticed there was a ring of armed guards around the gathering. Other Jones hardliners were hustling latecomers into the meeting.

A weary Jones finally came and sat in his regular chair. He seemed tired and even disorientated. His words on the tape recording made that afternoon were slurred. But the cult leader knew exactly what he wanted. "How very much I've loved you. How very much I've tried my best to give you a good life." Jones was speaking in the past tense; already he considered them dead. He went on to say that Ryan's plane was smoldering in the jungle. Even as he was speaking, Jones explained, Paraguayan paratroopers armed with automatic weapons were boarding their transports and preparing to attack the settlement and massacre every person. Children, said Jones, would be tortured. To protect them from this dreadful fate, the children would have to die first. Then one brave woman stood up and pleaded with the leader, but other cultists seized the microphone and shouted her down.

As Jones exhorted suicide, his well-drilled medical team swung into action. A large drum of Kool-Aid was produced. It had been used in drills before, but this was no drill. Schacht had mixed it with potassium cyanide, valium, the surgical sedative chloral hydrate, and potassium chloride. (The latter was designed to stop the heart and is used in the triumvirate of drugs deployed to execute prisoners by lethal injection.)

Parents were ordered to approach the station with their children. Nurses filled needleless syringes with the mixture and squirted it into the infants' mouths. Some resisted and several nurses would descend on these children and hold their jaws open to administer the drugs.

This is the most shocking part of the tapes. A low murmur of concern escalated into a cacophony of terrorized anguish as the children began to froth at the mouth and convulse in their death throes. Other children saw what was happening and desperately tried to escape. Naturally, some parents were caught up in the hysteria and refused to hand over their babies. Jones tried to soothe them, "Mother, mother, mother please… Don't do this," he said, before losing his temper and telling them to get it done.

There were 287 children killed on that terrible November day. Many had known no other life than Jonestown. And while the children were fed out of needles, most of the adults were told to line up at other stations. Here the poisonous concoction was poured into plastic cups.

Many of the members thought at first that it was just another drill. That was until one young man staggered onto the stage and collapsed against a supporting beam as his breathing became a desperate constricted whistling as his throat closed up. Hysteria almost broke out only to be suppressed by violent threats.

The process went on and the Temple members drank the poison and then staggered off into the field where they began to experience trouble breathing as their

ABOVE **In total 909 people committed suicide in Jonestown. Here, airtight coffins await shipment from Guyana back to the USA.**

entire systems broke down with cyanide-induced collapse. Moving among the bodies were Doctor Schacht and head nurse Phyllis Chaikin. They were checking for a pulse. Also moving among the dead were Jones's henchmen. They hauled the bodies off out of the way, placing them in neat concentric rows. This allowed more room for the next wave of suicides.

Not that all who died were suicides. Any who seemed reluctant were seized and hauled toward the vats where the posioned Kool-Aid was poured down their throats. Nurses armed with hypodermic needles pounced on many others, including the aged, and injected the lethal mix straight into the circulatory system.

Gradually the circle of guards—some armed with crossbows, others with firearms—drew tighter until there was nobody left to kill, though some had escaped the dragnet and were hiding at the jungle fringes or in hidey-holes within the settlement. All these survivors reported a gradual diminution of anguished voices and death rattles.

Although it is not exactly certain what happened, it seems from the film taken the following day that Jones's enforcers stacked their weapons neatly next to the pavilion before retiring to the leader's hut where they all congratulated each other on a job well done.

With a final "Hurrah!" they toasted each other and downed a final deadly drink. But the messianic madman who ordered this slaughter, the Reverend Jim Jones, was too cowardly to take this gruesome way out. He had a crony give him a relatively painless death with a shot to the head.

Thankfully, the Peoples Temple pretty much died with its leader. There was no collapse of the world order. Capitalism did not disappear as a result of "revolutionary suicide." Jones's deluded imaginings only brought about the needless death of hundreds of innocent people.

The Zealots

A "zealot" is now seen as one who has a fanatical belief in their religion. The Sicarii were a group of Zealots, a fanatical Jewish cult who first came to prominence in the Jewish Revolt (66–74 CE). They were fierce fighters who were feared even by the Romans. They were named after their daggers, the sicae, which they would pull from their cloaks to assassinate Romans and Jews alike. They seized the fortress at Masada and this was the last stronghold to fall to the Romans while they were putting down the savage revolt. Instead of surrendering to the Romans and beginning a life of slavery the leaders decided that the 960 Sicarii should all die. Since Judaism condemned suicide, lots were drawn and those who were chosen slit the throats of the other Zealots before handing over the dagger so they too could be killed. That meant only the last man would actually commit suicide, although all the others went to their deaths voluntarily.

RIGHT **Simon the Zealot, one of Christ's apostles, may have been a member of this sect.**

ORDER OF THE SOLAR TEMPLE

Little was known of this shadowy cult until a wave of mass suicides and murders erupted in secluded towns in Europe and Canada. Chalets were burned down and scores of immolated corpses were found in the smoldering ruins. Peaceful communities were rocked with the realization that a seemingly harmless fringe religious group harbored fanatical leaders bent on killing their entire flock.

While, as we shall see, Heaven's Gate members thought they could catch a spaceship after committing suicide, the members of the Solar Temple believed that if they were incinerated, after death they would be reincarnated on a planet orbiting the star Sirius. It appears that most members of Heaven's Gate went happily to their death; not so all the members of the Solar Temple. At least a quarter of the dead were killed against their will by pistol shots to the head, asphyxiation by plastic bag, or a forcefully administered overdose of sleeping pills. A postmortem of one teenager's corpse found a broken wrist, testifying to his desperate fight for survival.

The International Chivalric Order Solar Tradition, to give the movement its full title, was founded by Luc Jouret (1947–94) in 1984. It superseded The Foundation Golden Way, led by Joseph Di Mambro (1924–94). Di Mambro was convinced he was the reincarnation of a member of the Knights Templar who had last lived in the 14th century. He was also convinced that his daughter was the pure "Cosmic Child."

As in many cults, members were asked to sign over their worldly possessions and renounce their day-to-day concerns while refusing to communicate with friends and family. Solar Temple groups were organized in Quebec and Switzerland as well as other countries. These lodges had altars, rituals, and costumes hearkening back to the Middle Ages. Members would progress through each stage of "enlightenment" in ceremonies which included expensive purchases such as jewelry and regalia as well as the payment of hefty initiation fees. During ceremonies members wore Templar robes and were awed to hold a sword which Di Mambro said was an authentic Templar artifact, given to him centuries earlier in his previous life.

Closeted in their fantasy world, Jouret and Di Mambro made claims that became more and more delusional. Jouret believed that he was a reincarnation of Jesus Christ, and the two men convinced their followers that after death they would lead them to a planet orbiting Sirius. While these spiritual aims were suitably lofty, Jouret had much baser drives. Before each ceremony he had sex with one of the female cult members.

Gradually, in late 1994, the law began to catch up with the cult. Jouret was convicted for illegal possession of a firearm, and Antonio Dutoit, a disenchanted member who worked on the cult's accounts, tried to flee with his wife and infant child. But they were not going to escape so easily, and the infant's parents were killed before they could report financial irregularities they had found in the cult account to the increasingly hostile authorities. And Jouret's revenge did not finish there. Three-month-old Emmanuel, the couple's son, was sacrificed, repeatedly stabbed with a sharpened stake, as Di Mambro had declared him to be the Antichrist.

Nonetheless, the net was closing quickly on the cult, as being based in several locations around the world, a number of governments began to investigate its shady goings-on. This precipitated a wave of suicides, as the members were persuaded that an Armageddon-like natural catastrophe was imminent and they had to transit to another world before that occurred.

Soon after the murder of baby Emmanuel, Di Mambro held a last supper with his 12 closest disciples on October 2, 1994. It is likely that during this conference the blueprint for the program of suicides was laid down and two days later on October 4th members began to kill themselves. Some of the suicides occurred in villages in Switzerland, while others died in a pleasant ski resort called Morin Heights in Quebec, Canada. The first the authorities knew of these tragedies was often when their fire departments were summoned to the burning cult residences.

ABOVE A Quebec police officer holds cult paraphernalia recovered from the house in Saint-Casimir where five members of the Order of the Solar Temple committed suicide.

The method of death was not always the same: 15 of the inner circle, the "awakened," died by poison; 30 "immortals" were smothered or shot; and at least eight, the "traitors," were killed seemingly against their will. Some individuals had as many as eight bullets lodged in their skull.

In Switzerland, many of the victims were found in a secret underground chapel with mirrors and other items of Templar symbolism. The bodies were dressed in the order's ceremonial robes and were in a circle, feet together, heads outward and covered with plastic bags. They had all been shot in the head.

Most of the properties were torched in line with the cult's belief that they would end up in the Sirius system quicker if they cremated their now soulless cadavers. Timed incendiary devices incinerated the lodges.

Although the two leaders were dead, it was obvious that they still had a deathly hold over the remaining cult members. Close to the winter solstice in 1995, 16 of the remaining group disappeared from their homes. Many left goodbye notes to their loved ones. They were later found dead in a remote forest in the Vercors Mountains of France; four of the children had defense wounds and one adult had had her jaw fractured as she tried to flee. Most of the dead had sedatives in their system. The French authorities concluded that the last surviving members, a policeman and an architect, had poured petrol over their family's corpses, set them on fire, and shot each other before they fell into the flames.

BELOW **The burned remains of Luc Jouret's residence in Morin Heights, Canada. On October 4, members of the cult "transitioned" before the house was set on fire.**

Once again in Saint-Casimir, Quebec, five additional adult members and three teenage children apparently tried to commit suicide on the day of the 1997 spring equinox. The attempt failed due to faulty equipment. The teenage sons and daughter of one of the couples convinced their parents that they wanted to live. They were allowed to leave, while the adults made their second, this time successful, attempt to burn down the house with themselves in it. Four of their bodies were arranged in the form of a cross. The teens were found drugged and disoriented, but otherwise safe, in a nearby building. A note was found there which described the group belief that death on earth leads to a transit to a new planet where their lives would continue.

ABOVE **A former member of the Order of the Solar Temple explains how it was necessary to commit suicide to ascend to a higher order of existence.**

The police decided not to charge the three teenage survivors of the Saint-Casimir mass suicide with arson. Although they had triggered the incendiary device, they were under the influence of sedatives at the time, and had been psychologically affected by living with members of the Solar Temple group. Other factors considered by the prosecutor were that they tried to persuade the adults to not commit suicide and chose life for themselves.

MOST OF THE PROPERTIES WERE TORCHED IN LINE WITH THE CULT'S BELIEFS THAT THEY WOULD END UP IN THE SIRIUS SYSTEM QUICKER IF THEY CREMATED THEIR NOW SOULLESS CADAVERS. TIMED INCENDIARY DEVICES INCINERATED THE LODGES.

HEAVEN'S GATE

On March 26, 1997, a remarkable phone call was made to police in San Diego: a member of Heaven's Gate had ventured into the cult's rented mansion in Rancho Santa Fe and found 39 corpses. When police attended they found the most orderly mass suicide in cult history. All of the dead were lying peacefully on bunk beds. Dressed in black trousers and shirts with white or black socks, they all were wearing brand-new black Nike runners and had their hands crossed peacefully over their breasts. Emblazoned on their breasts were "Heaven's Gate Away Team" patches. There were no signs of violence, and only two had plastic bags over their heads, hinting at how they had died. Most were covered with a purple shawl measuring three feet by three feet. Not wanting to make things

BELOW A member of Heaven's Gate lies where he died in 1997. Each member wore identical clothing and was covered with a purple blanket.

difficult for the authorities, all of the dead had IDs placed next to their corpses. Those who wore glasses placed them with folded arms next to their IDs.

The members had all "transited" to a spaceship trailing the 15-mile (24-kilometer) wide Hale–Bopp Comet then traversing the summer skies over the American West Coast.

The first 15 had committed suicide on March 23, 1997, the time when Hale–Bopp was closest to earth. The cult members had imbibed a lethal mixture of phenobarbital mixed with apple sauce and pudding, and washed down with copious amounts of vodka.

Phenobarbital is commonly used to prevent fits in epileptics, but when given as an overdose it depresses the central nervous system and slows the bodily functions. It can shut down kidneys and lead to brain death. A lethal dose of this drug is 100 micrograms per milliliter and cult members were found with up to 164 micrograms in each milliliter of blood. Blood alcohol levels averaged about 0.11 percent, showing that all were effectively drunk at the time of death. Remembering that many of the corpses had lain unattended for up to four days before the autopsies, it is likely that the initial levels were much higher. As the county coroner explained, some were in a more "advanced" state of decomposition than the others, and the last to die must have noticed a deathly stench beginning to emanate from those who had gone before. None had life-threatening illnesses and if they hadn't been dead, all 39 would have been in good health. For some reason, all had packed their bags and placed them neatly at the foot of their beds, and each had a five-dollar note and some coins in their pockets.

It seems that plastic bags were tied around the necks of the cultists to speed the process through asphyxiation, although these bags were removed once they were dead. The dead were then placed on bunks and mattresses, and their faces were covered with the purple shawls.

On the following day, another 15 cult members went peacefully to their deaths using the same methodology. Then on March 25th the final nine also went to their heavenly rendezvous. The last two to die still had plastic bags on their heads. All had a non-gender-specific buzz cut and eight of the 18 male members had been castrated. But how did such a gruesome gathering ever come to pass?

The Coming of the Comet

On November 14, 1996, a seemingly innocent phone call sparked what would be one of the worst mass suicides in American history. An amateur astronomer by the name of Chuck Shramek (1950–2000) called Art Bell's radio show, *Coast to Coast*. The show delighted in discussing the weird and wonderful, and Art was always keen to hear of his listeners' paranormal experiences. Chuck did not disappoint and claimed that he

ABOVE **Hale-Bopp Comet. If you looked closely, according to Applewhite, you could see a spacecraft piloted by Bonnie Nettles come to collect "transitioned" souls.**

had taken a photo of the approaching Hale–Bopp comet. Trailing in the comet's wake was an object that looked like a spaceship. It was shaped like Saturn and appeared to be bigger than the earth!

Not letting truth get in the way of a good story, Bell invited Courtney Brown, the head of the Atlanta Farsight Institute, onto his show. This man believed in "remote viewing" and claimed that three of his psychics had made contact with the strange metallic object, which was in fact an interstellar craft manned by aliens. (In reality, the photo was eventually released to the press, and the object proved to be a misidentified star.)

Most who heard this interview would have dismissed it as so much nonsense. But this was not the case for Marshall "Herff" Applewhite, the leader of a small cult known as Heaven's Gate. In fact, the news report was just what he was waiting for. Pulling several thousand dollars out of the cult kitty, he took a devotee member down to Oceanside Photo and Telescope shop in San Diego and bought a large astronomical telescope. While not proficient in its use, Applewhite had a look through the viewfinder and determined that there was in fact a large spaceship behind the approaching comet. What's more it was crewed by the intergalactic soul of his spiritual partner, Bonnie Nettles (1927–85), who had died during the previous decade. She was swinging by the earth so that she could pick up the rest of the cult members and take them to the next level. All the members had to do was liberate their souls by destroying the "physical containers" or "vehicles," as they called their bodies.

There was a sense of urgency. The cult leader believed he was dying of cancer and had to transition to a new phase of existence before his own "vehicle" died. As a result, the other members of the cult were similarly anxious to be off, as they could not imagine life without their beloved leader. Applewhite would give them all a "boarding pass" for an intergalactic jaunt to oblivion.

A Born Leader

There was nothing in Marshall Applewhite's background that would mark his potential as a crazed sociopath determined to lead his fanatical followers in a suicide pact. His friends called him "Herff," and he was well known for his sense of humor and his musical abilities. Herff's favorite act was an "elephant walk" that made everyone fall about with laughter. Funny and charismatic, he was able to amuse people with a fine sense of comic timing or entrance them with his beautiful singing voice. During his school years Marshall was a "chronic overachiever" who was president of everything, according to his sister. Possessed of some charisma, with his penetrating bright eyes he also had the gift of the gab and could convince any audience that he was the right man for the job. Several of his early associates mentioned that the young Christian was a born leader. Affectionate and popular, Marshall "Herff" Applewhite seemed to have it all.

However, there were dark shadows emerging. Applewhite was the son of a Presbyterian minister who moved from place to place every three years, founding new churches. This rootless existence meant Herff had to leave friends behind, throwing up emotions that a young adolescent found difficult to deal with. He also had homosexual urges, something that his puritan father would have been disgusted with if he had ever heard about it. Applewhite senior made sure his family stayed on the straight and narrow. Sex was for procreation and not for pleasure. This message would have been hammered home time after time as the family moved around the Bible Belt of Texas, spreading the Lord's word.

Throughout his thirties, during the 1960s, Applewhite lived a very conventional life. He settled down, got married and had two children. He played starring roles in stage musicals in Colorado and Texas. He was the choir director at St. Mark's Episcopal Church in Houston. In addition to teaching at the university, he sang 15 roles with Houston Grand Opera.

Then, in the 1970s, things began to fall apart. Unable to suppress his homosexual urges, the music professor at the University of St. Thomas in Houston embarked upon a furtive affair with one of his male students. Although the university fired him for this reason, they cited that Applewhite's tenure was terminated due to "health problems of an emotional nature." Increasingly unstable, he left his family and checked into a hospital to be cured of his homosexual urges. He may have been suffering anxiety attacks and heart palpitations; no one is really sure.

What is certain is that he met a 44-year-old nurse, Bonnie Lu Nettles, who would change his life forever and take him well beyond the bounds of reality.

The middle-aged mother was also becoming increasingly delusional during the early 1970s and became convinced that a 19th-century monk called Brother Francis was speaking to her and issuing instructions. She ran many séances and was told by

ABOVE **Applewhite and Nettles. Their fantasies began to intertwine until they became reality. When Nettles died, Applewhite's thoughts turned to mass suicide.**

several fortune tellers that she was destined to meet a tall man with light hair. Applewhite fitted the bill.

Nettles was convinced that the two were destined for greatness and would found a religion that would uncover greater truths. So the two deluded spiritualists cut ties with their families and began a rootless existence roaming around Texas carrying out petty thefts while trying to recruit members to their cult. They changed their names, first to Bo and Peep and then to Ti and Do. Their petty crimes included taking credit cards from family members and "forgetting" to return hire cars. It was for this latter crime that Applewhite was arrested and did a brief stint in jail.

During this period the two studied various religious tracts and bits of New Age bunkum and began to develop their own religious ideology. They discovered that they were in fact "The Two" from the Book of Revelation, that the world was about to end, and only extra-terrestrials in their unidentified flying objects (UFOs) could rescue humanity.

Their teachings came down to a simple idea: a soul could be perfected by following their program, and once a new level had been reached the individual could be resurrected or transformed into a new alien body that was immortal. Only by overcoming the base drives of human behavior could an individual evolve to the higher consciousness and be accepted into a new alien host. The metaphors of a caterpillar becoming a butterfly and Jesus's resurrection were offered as the cult's evidence for this process.

The two bombarded health food stores, yoga schools, and the early internet with their cosmic message, and gradually attracted a small following of desperate and needy individuals. They appealed to the gullible, but the combination of Applewhite's charisma and a generally supportive environment seemed attractive to many who sought some kind of meaning in their lives.

Once the members had been attracted to the cult, Applewhite and Nettles used the traditional methods to weld their followers to their crazy ideals. Members were encouraged to give up all of their worldly wealth. Sex was a definite no-no, and all members wore shapeless and sexless clothes, giving up any adornments or personal fashion styles. Many male members were voluntarily castrated, allowing them to cast aside any earthly urges. Unlike most cult leaders, Applewhite actually practiced what he preached in sexual matters and he, too, was castrated. Given that it was his conflicted attitude to his latent homosexuality that was a key psychological motivation for Applewhite's spirituality, perhaps he welcomed the clarity this procedure gave him.

The cult moved around through different states and locations, which made it difficult for concerned family members to track their loved ones. Rigorous meditation and work schedules along with strict controls over diet and free time ensured that no member was given a chance to question the increasingly strident propaganda of the cult.

BELOW **Heaven's Gate cult members posing for a photo at the seaside. Unlike in many cults, members were free to leave at any time.**

Time to Go

Nettles died in 1985, but when she did not undergo any metamorphic transformation, Applewhite shifted his ideas in a new and dangerous direction. Heaven's Gate began to believe that their bodies were "vehicles" that could be left at will and moved to a new state. It appears that Applewhite toyed with the idea of suicide by violence, and to that end he purchased a veritable arsenal of pistols and rifles. The cult members, who were genuinely peaceful individuals, were shocked by this idea and Applewhite had to hatch a new scheme.

In 1995 the cult took out a lease on a palatial mansion in Rancho Santa Fe. They were quiet and didn't distract their neighbors, although a large internet-servicing business was run from the premises. Finally, Applewhite got the sign he was waiting for—the radio report of the approaching comet. The cult leader and one of his most trusted acolytes purchased a large telescope and were able to confirm that behind the particularly large comet was a spaceship.

Do, as Applewhite was known, confirmed that this vast ship was being crewed by none other than Ti (Nettles), who had taken on an extraterrestrial form. She was swinging by to pick up the select few, so they all had to get ready to leave planet earth.

The cultists prepared for their transition. Polite messages were sent to all of their clients terminating business arrangements. Each member was then filmed giving what they called their "final exit statement." Taken over several days these chilling videos are remarkable for the lovely surrounds of Rancho Santa Fe. While birds sing in the background and trees rustle in the breeze, 39 individuals describe how they are welcoming suicide. One thing stands out: they are all remarkably cheerful.

Many speak of how Do and Ti give their lives meaning and were instantly recognizable as saviors. They progress cheerfully to their deaths, demonstrating the absolute hold Applewhite had over these lost souls.

Herff himself gives one last lecture, trying to attract adherents from beyond the grave. In the footage his slightly demonic, staring eyes gaze at the camera while he speaks, a rapt audience of totally brainwashed cult members before him. Embarrassingly, as Applewhite pans the camera over his vacant-looking audience he gets some of their names wrong. Only 20 are in the room, all of them about to die for his demented beliefs, but Christ reincarnated can't show even a modicum of respect and get their names right.

His final dissertation shows the typically convoluted thinking of such gurus. Applewhite explains that they are committing suicide because the kingdom of God is giving them a chance at a new life. To remain alive in their "vehicles" would in fact be committing suicide!

RIGHT Applewhite's mesmeric stare convinced many that he was a divine messenger. Here, he issues individuals with a "boarding pass" to immortality.

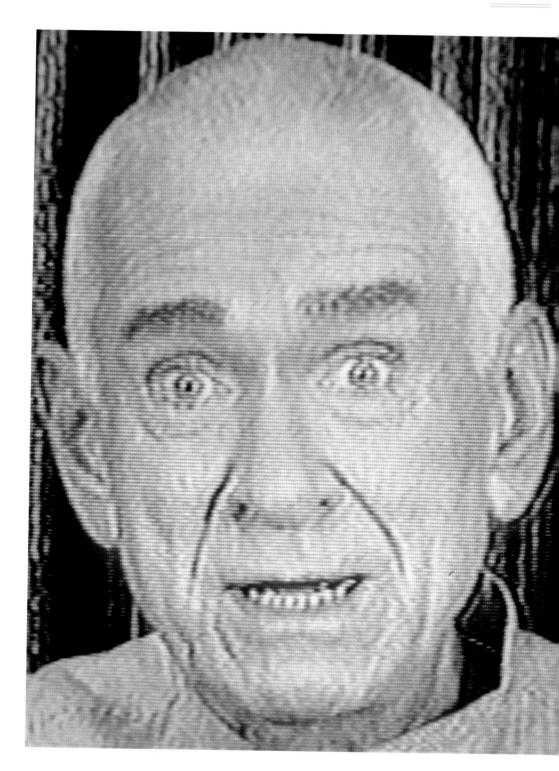

ABOVE **Emergency services remove corpses from the Heaven's Gate compound. Those who had died in the first wave of suicides were beginning to rot.**

Applewhite speaks with total conviction, and his disciples seem beyond the ability to question him. They have entered what is a psychiatric syndrome called folie à deux, where a shared delusion grows as more people buy into the concept and build on it. These ideas would not stand up to any logic once removed from the support network of delusion that a cult provides.

The cult believed that evil space aliens called Luciferians repressed all of humanity and prevented them from ascending to what they called the "next level." To attain "human individual metamorphism," all earthly concerns had to be shed. Helping the members was the "tone," where members would concentrate for hours on the ringing of a tuning fork, excluding all other thoughts. Another rule was to reduce all talk to the barest minimum. For days, all communication was "unnecessary," and they could only say, "Yes", "No," or "Don't know" in answer to a brief question. Otherwise, small handwritten notes were used.

Among the delusions was the belief that Applewhite was the Second Coming of Jesus and that Nettles was the heavenly father. So the thinking went, Jesus had actually left his "vehicle" two thousand years ago and had now returned in the guise of Applewhite to guide his students to the next level. Once the followers of Heaven's Gate had ascended, no others anywhere else would be able to join them until the next age, though in that regard, Applewhite did give us all one last chance. If we studied his teachings we, too, could be given a "boarding pass" to the next passing interstellar machine.

The cult members quietly recorded their last messages, packed their bags and cleaned the palatial villa until it was "spotless," according to the local police. Then they downed their vodka and ate their pudding.

Just before the last suicides a message was sent to a former cult member, Rio DiAngelo, who had left because he could not abide the monastic lifestyle. (Any cult member was free to leave whenever they wanted, one unique positive aspect of the group.) The package contained two videos and a letter containing an ominous last message. He hurried to Rancho Santa Fe and found the macabre and by this time noisome scene of 39 dead cultists lying peacefully in their beds. He had the foresight to take a camera with him and videoed his grisly discovery before calling the police.

Initially, the police thought all of the dead cult members were male, as the loose clothes and crew cuts made them appear asexual. They urgently began tracking down other members to prevent more suicides. Robert Nichols, a 58-year-old ex-roadie beat them to the punch, killing himself in his trailer on March 28, 1997, leaving a note saying that he was looking forward to meeting his friends on the next level. As he asphyxiated himself in a plastic bag he also covered himself with a purple cloth.

Just over a month later, on May 6th, two more members sought to "ascend" in a Holiday Inn Express room near Las Vegas; 54-year-old Wayne Cooke managed to kill himself, but Charles Humphreys was resuscitated, though not for long. Soon after, the 55-year-old managed to kill himself by feeding his exhaust pipe into a tent and tying a plastic bag over his head.

Police investigations revealed that Applewhite had committed suicide with the second batch of fifteen members. His autopsy revealed that he was in fact free of the cancer which had so haunted his adherents and precipitated the slaughter.

THE CULT BELIEVED THAT EVIL SPACE ALIENS CALLED LUCIFERIANS REPRESSED ALL OF HUMANITY AND PREVENTED THEM FROM ASCENDING TO WHAT THEY CALLED THE "NEXT LEVEL." TO ATTAIN "HUMAN INDIVIDUAL METAMORPHISM," ALL EARTHLY CONCERNS HAD TO BE SHED.

CHAPTER 3

CULTS THAT KILL

SOME RELIGIONS AND CULTS BELIEVE THAT to attain spiritual fulfillment, you must treat your fellow creatures with dignity and respect. Others have believed that the path to enlightenment involves the wholesale slaughter of their fellow man. The Assassins trained devoted killers who would dispatch political enemies before welcoming violent retribution, which guaranteed a place in paradise. We may consider such groups as unhinged and mad. But their followers held sincere beliefs that turned them into killer cults.

THE AZTECS

The Aztecs excelled in blood sacrifice. Over several hundred years they developed bloody cults that had one goal, to sacrifice anything with a pulse. Small furry animals, young men and women, old crones—none was exempt. Anything with a beating heart was fair game to the Aztecs (or Mexica, as they called themselves) in their efforts to assuage their bloodthirsty gods. If the sacrificial victim happened to endure agonizing torture along the way, then all the better, too.

You could call the Aztec blood sacrifice the ultimate crazy cult. You'd call it something else if you were the one being hauled up the side of a Mesoamerican pyramid to have your chest torn open with an obsidian blade before your still-beating heart was ripped out and offered to Huitzilopochtli, their god of war.

BELOW **The Mexica settled on Lake Texcoco and brought their gods with them. Soon they had built an empire dedicated to Huitzilopochtli, the god of war.**

The Mexica were remarkably religious people and always seemed to have some god in need of sacrifice. Eighteen months out of 18 in the Aztec calendar involved human sacrifice of some kind. Prisoners of war, women, young boys and girls, infants, slaves, and animals all seem likely to have been killed. The only ones who didn't have to suffer this fate were the ruling elite, or grown men, unless they were captured in battle by an enemy state.

There was one time, however, when everybody could relax. Prisoners, slaves, and the others likely to be killed could at least have five days of the year where they knew that they wouldn't have to worry. The period between February 9th and 13th was a time for doing absolutely nothing. To avoid bad luck, everybody stayed in their homes and did not do any business.

The Mexica actually considered that they were doing their sacrificial victims a big favor when they were sacrificed by one of the many cults—if not in this life, then definitely in the afterlife. According to the Aztec (and Mesoamerican) worldview, the circumstances in which people died determined the type of afterlife they enjoyed. Basically, the more painful and horrible the death, the better the afterlife an individual could expect.

If you were unlucky enough to die peacefully in your own bed surrounded by your loved ones, you were doomed to wander the afterlife enduring trials and tribulations before you finally settled in a somber and gloomy underworld with little joy or color. However, if you were fortunate enough to die in battle with your head cloven in two by an obsidian-lined war club, or maybe on top of a temple with your rib cage broken open and your still pulsing heart extracted before your eyes, or if you were a woman who died after an agonizing failed childbirth lasting days, in fact you had experienced a good death and your soul went straight to the second-highest level of heaven. One belief was that warriors killed while fighting became hummingbirds serving the great sun god. A dead infant immediately went to the highest plain in heaven as the very young were considered to be pure. This may explain why such huge numbers of Mesoamericans went peacefully to their deaths even though they must have sometimes outnumbered their captives. Where this unique and to us perverted worldview came from is difficult to ascertain, but hallucinogenic mushrooms were often ingested at religious events, as it was believed they gave the participants a window into the divine. One group of kings witnessed 80,000 human sacrifices at the consecration of the Templo Mayor and then feasted on magic mushrooms. It can only be wondered what their mental state would have been after such an ordeal.

The Mexica obviously had a lot of time on their hands and at least 52 gods and goddesses in their pantheon. Each of these gods had their own cult worshippers. Some of these were quite important, but equally a lot of them were pretty trivial. Why

any society would require a goddess of gentle breezes or a god of sexual misdeeds is not immediately obvious. Nevertheless, the Aztecs felt an overwhelming need to satisfy all of their major and minor gods with a staggering number of sacrifices involving a huge array of violent deaths. People were beaten, decapitated, burned, starved, drowned, eaten, buried alive, shot with arrows, and eviscerated.

ABOVE Throughout Central and South America civilizations had practiced human sacrifice for thousands of years. This depiction dates to the 16th century.

The Tradition of Sacrifice

The Aztecs inherited a tradition of sacrifice going back millennia to the earlier Maya and Toltec societies. These cultures practiced auto-sacrifice which, while not deadly, was extremely painful. Sharp objects such as quills from animals, stingray barbs, and thorns on knotted strings would be used to pierce the penis or tongue before they were pulled through, creating exquisite pain which summoned the spirits before the resulting cascade of blood would be sprinkled over altars or in fields to guarantee fertility. The Maya often collected the blood on paper, which was then burned upon an altar like incense to summon a deity. Human sacrifice was quite common, prisoners of war would often be tortured, and deposed leaders were symbolically sacrificed to demonstrate that a city state had been conquered. Neither did the Maya sacrifice just anyone; they believed in quality over quantity and usually restricted their sacrifices to noblemen or captured kings. Nor were sacrificial victims always killed; sometimes they merely had their fingernails and toenails pulled out to generate

the desired quantity of blood. One ruler showed his contempt for an enemy he had killed by wearing the luckless individual's fingernails as a necklace. Warfare was largely restricted to feuds between royal houses.

The Mexica Tlatoani (Emperor) Tlacaelel made human sacrifice a demonstration of the power of his empire and linked the status of his and his successors' rule to the amount of blood they were able to shed. Sacrifice became a political rather than a religious statement, and under the Aztec regime, bloodletting reached unprecedented heights. At the same time, the Mexica did continue with the tradition of auto-sacrifice, with one unsuccessful Tlatoani seeking to atone for a military defeat by piercing his own calves, earlobes, and shins with a sharpened jaguar bone.

Huitzilopochtli, being the chief god within the Mexica pantheon, received the most human sacrifices throughout the year. During at least five months of the year people were sacrificed to satisfy this god's desires. The fifteenth month was wholly dedicated to mass sacrifices of prisoners of war to this god. Huitzipochtli's role as sun god made him the Aztec insurance policy. It was believed that blood sacrificed to him guaranteed the sun would rise. Every day during this month at

ABOVE A giant statue of Tlaloc, the Aztec god of rain. The Mexica believed that crying children had to be sacrificed to ensure bountiful crops.

least one person was sacrificed to him, just in case.

Huitzilopochtli was the tribal deity of the Aztecs and had to be appeased to guarantee success to the Mexica in war. He was mostly associated with the sun at the zenith and with warfare and the burning of towns, and was often represented as a fire-breathing serpent. The chief aim of the Aztec state was to use the campaigning season to catch prisoners and bring them back for sacrifice to this god. An Aztec ruler measured his success by the number of victims he was able to muster for sacrifice on the fifteenth month in November and December. This celebration month was known as Toxcatl, during which captives and slaves were brought forth and slain ceremoniously. Every 52 years, the Mexica feared the world would end. Under Tlacaelel Aztecs believed that they could give strength to Huitzilopochtli with human blood and thereby postpone the end of the world, at least for another 52 years.

When the Aztecs sacrificed people to Huitzilopochtli, the victim was stripped of any ornaments and placed on a large sacrificial stone facing upward with his head and limbs held steady by priests. Then a senior priest—who would often be dressed as, and therefore symbolically identified with, the god—would cut through the abdomen with an obsidian or flint blade. The heart would be torn out, still beating and held toward the sky to give sustenance to the sun god in his passage across the sky. Blood from the wound was collected in a basin, and the smell of the blood combined with burning incense to waft into the sky, further fortifying Huitzilopochtli. The body would be carried away and either cremated or given to the warrior responsible for the capture of the victim. If given to the warrior, he would cut the body into pieces and send them to important people and his relatives as an offering while using some of the pieces for ritual cannibalism.

Sometimes the flayed flesh of the deceased would be worn by his captor so that he could acquire some of the victim's vigor and fertility. Warriors gained prestige within Mexica society depending on the number of prisoners they brought back for sacrifice. Higher status was reflected in their clothing and their role in festivals.

The Aztecs were an agricultural people, so rain was incredibly important for the community's well-being. The Aztecs believed that if sacrifices were not given to Tlaloc, the rain god, rain would not come and crops would not grow. (The fact that the Templo Mayor was topped by a shrine to Tlaloc and a shrine to Huitzilopochtli, the god of war and the sun, shows that these three issues were the key concern of this society.) Children were seen as suitable for this sacrifice, but on one condition: they had to be crying. The remains of 42 children have been found in the archaeological record around the Templo Mayor, and almost all of the children had ulcerated teeth and gums or other unpleasant infections, meaning they would have been in constant pain and would probably have cried continuously. Tlaloc required the tears of the young to wet the earth. As a result, if children did not cry, the priests would sometimes tear off the children's nails before the ritual sacrifice. The number of children killed would have been huge, and there are estimates that one in five children surviving childbirth may have been sacrificed.

Children were sacrificed throughout the year. In the first month they were ritually killed as a sacrifice to water deities, and the flesh was ritually eaten, often by the parents. The earth goddess was worshipped by raising a young girl for several months in the guise of the deity before being sacrificed through decapitation. The skin was then flayed and worn by a priest in honor of the goddess and used to conduct ceremonies within the earth goddess's temple and the corn god's shrine. It was believed that by wearing the skin of the goddess, the priest was able to capture part of the deity's soul and transfer the mystical powers to the environment. The rotting skin would also fill the temple with an unholy stench and after about three weeks would reach such a stage of decomposition that it would fall off the priest. Similarly, the waters of Lake Texcoco were blessed each year with the blood of young boys and girls who had had their throats slashed, and the life-giving elixir was sprinkled on the water to guarantee fertility. River spirits were appeased by having six-year-old children, with their faces painted blue and their hands bound behind them, tossed into the waterways where the spirits resided. Children's hearts were also thrown into rivers, creeks, and aqueducts. In another ceremony children's blood was mixed with cornmeal and made into an image of Huitzilopochtli before being eaten by nobles and the Tlatoani as a kind of cannibal's gingerbread man.

The Feast of Toxcatl

Arguably the most important god in the Mexica pantheon was Tezcatlipoca. Given a huge step pyramid all to himself, dominating a quarter of the sacred precinct, he was god of night, sorcery, destiny, and the north. It was believed that he created war to ensure a constant supply of food and drink for the gods. Known as "the enemy," he was responsible for all discord within the world. Most importantly, Tezcatlipoca knew the fate of each man, and only through intercession by this powerful god could an individual's or nation's fate be altered. Tezcatlipoca was seen as all-powerful and all-knowing, and a Mexica translation of one his titles could read

BELOW Tezcatlipoca, the god of chaos. A young man lived as this deity for a year, enjoying unimaginable carnal delights, before he was sacrificed.

as "He whose slaves we are." A more direct translation of his name was "black obsidian," the material which sacrificial knives and most weapons were made of.

One of the most important rituals on the Aztec calendar was the great feast of Toxcatl, which took place on April 23rd as the days were lengthening. It began a year beforehand, and involved sacrificing Tezcatlipoca to himself. A particularly handsome young man would be selected to take upon himself the mantle of divinity. For one year he lived in the temple, treated like a god and waited on hand and foot by powerful Aztec lords and attending priests. He also was able to enjoy four of the most comely maids, selected from noble young women, whose aim was to satisfy his every emotional and physical desire. These brides represented the goddess of flowers, the goddess of young corn, the goddess of fertility, and the goddess of salt. He was able to leave the temple under close escort and wander the streets of Tenochtitlan (the site of modern-day Mexico City), where he was worshipped and adored by the people.

But being part of an Aztec ceremony, he knew the good times could not last. On the feast day of Toxcatl, the young man was taken from the temple and brought to a hilltop overlooking Lake Texcoco. He said farewell to his bride-goddesses and walked up to a small temple where, as soon as he crossed the threshold, he was seized by the priests and had his living heart ripped from his torso. The altar and threshold were painted with the god's blood and as soon as all life signs ceased, a new "god" was selected and proclaimed.

The festival of the god of fire, Xiuhtecuhtli, one of the original deities of the one-time wandering Mexica, ended the calendar year, so it was important that it went off with a bang. Although the modern New Year is celebrated with a wide range of fireworks, the Aztecs celebrated by burning small furry animals, frogs, lizards, and, of course, newly married couples.

Xiuhtecuhtli was always in the minds of the Mexica, and the first morsel of any cooked meal was tossed into the flames to thank the god for his generous gift. But in the 18th month of the Aztec year, it was more than morsels that were thrown into the fire. The priests began by building a wickerwork representation of their god in front of his temple and setting it alight. Young children would capture animals and offer them to the priest, who would toss them into the fire. Then specially selected, recently wed couples were given a taste of the action. Dressed in elaborate ceremonial clothes representing Xiuhtecuhtli, they were tossed into the fires that raged upon the deity's altars. As they flailed about in agony, the priests watched them carefully and, just as they seemed to be about to die, hauled them out of the flames with large metal hooks, splaying both bride and groom across the sacrificial stone to tear out their barely beating hearts. Xiuhtecuhtli was able to feast not only on the living bodies of his offerings, but also their life force in the form of the hearts and blood that were offered to him in this particularly nasty ritual.

ABOVE The huge step pyramids often had channels carved next to the steps to allow rivers of blood to flow down to the soil.

Pyramid Temples

Other rituals, those marking the planting season and the harvest, were dedicated to one of the oldest gods, the goddess of fertility Teteoinnan. The antiquity of the goddess can be attested to by the fact that throughout North, Central, and South America many indigenous cultures worshipped a variation of this deity, and many had similar rituals. Some eastern and southwestern tribes of North America only practiced human sacrifice to honor their version of the earth mother, having abandoned other sacrificial rituals. The Aztec ritual was grisly in the extreme. At the height of the harvest festival, at midnight on August 21st, the woman who represented this goddess was decapitated by priests before being flayed. Her skin was then squeezed onto a young man who temporarily took on the best aspects of the deity. The skin from one thigh was removed from the flensed flesh and taken to the high priest of the corn goddess, who proceeded to wear it as a mask. The young man representing the earth mother then sacrificed four more victims before being banished from the empire, while the high priest deposited his mask at a far-flung part of the empire's territory, having worn it on the long journey there.

Operating in cahoots with the earth goddess was the corn temple, whose sacrifices were just as bloody. A young woman had her face painted yellow and red to represent ripened grain and her arms and legs were covered with bright feathers. Dancing for hours before the temple on the eve of the harvest festival, she then entered the building and was seized by a priest, who carried her on his back as if he was the sacrificial stone. Then another priest cut off the victim's head before tearing the heart from her young body.

The pyramid temples built by the Mesoamericans not only functioned as stages for sacrifice but were demonstrations of a city-state's prestige. The bigger the temple, the greater the power. Remodeled and rebuilt to get higher and higher on a regular basis, each new version of a temple was consecrated with ritual sacrifices. As in most areas, the Aztecs outdid their neighbors, with the greatest recorded mass sacrifice of prisoners staged by the all-conquering emperor Ahuizotl, when he'd finished building the Templo Mayor in the middle of the Sacred Precinct in Tenochtitlan.

Returning in 1488 from his victorious campaign subjugating states to the northeast, he and the army brought with them a huge train of captives. The men were dragged along with rope through the pierced septum of their noses while women and children were tied to wooden yokes. Other military expeditions had returned with captives from other regions, and subject allies had been ordered to provide slaves. In all, Ahuizotl had gathered 80,400 prisoners to be sacrificed at the inauguration of the Templo Mayor.

Client kings and enemies of the empire were invited to witness the ceremonies. Ahuizotl was determined to overawe any potential opposition, and the scale of his sacrifices achieved just that. The Tlatoani greeted his fellow rulers with great pomp and ceremony before the festivities began. Sitting atop the new, blindingly white temple before the shrines to Huitzilopochtli and Tlaloc, they all had a perfect view of the main plaza filled with the lines of captives awaiting execution. Hundreds of thousands of porters bearing tribute from the empire then descended upon the city, depositing unimaginable wealth at the foot of the temple before it was taken to huge warehouses throughout the city.

On the second day the sacrifices began. The temple rose 106 feet (32.3 m) above the city and the twin temples of the chief deities added another 56 feet (17 m). The captives, in huge lines stretching beyond the city limits, were herded up the 100 steps of the pyramid to meet their fate. At the top of the stairs they were seized by priests

AT THE HEIGHT OF THE HARVEST FESTIVAL, AT MIDNIGHT ON AUGUST 21ST, THE WOMAN WHO REPRESENTED THIS GODDESS WAS DECAPITATED BY PRIESTS BEFORE BEING FLAYED. HER SKIN WAS THEN SQUEEZED ONTO A YOUNG MAN WHO TEMPORARILY TOOK ON THE BEST ASPECTS OF THE DEITY.

and bent backward over the sacrificial stones so that their chests arched upward. A priest held each limb taut and with a practiced slash the kings and their priests sliced open the chest and pulled the beating heart out of each victim. The relay was endless and once one priest was too fatigued to continue another quickly replaced him to carry on the work. Each body spurted out several pints of blood, which soon ran over the lip of the platform and streamed down the sides of the temple. Rivers of blood ran down the temple and as they cooled great globules of the fluid formed into large clots. Some of the priests gathered the liquid in gourds and took it to different temples throughout the precinct, smearing the walls, idols, and even roofs. In the hot sun the blood began to ferment and rot, sending out a dreadful stench that covered the entire city with a foul miasma.

Things were only to get worse. The victims were thrown down the sides of the pyramid where teams of butchers dismembered and decapitated them. The heads were transported to the new skull rack built just for this ceremony. Some of the bodies were given to warriors for ritual cooking and consumption, but such was the amount of fresh steaming meat that it couldn't all be carted off to the pot. Relays were organized to haul the unwanted corpses and toss them into the surrounding lagoons and canals. So much flesh was dumped that it began to corrupt and rot, turning the once fresh water of Lake Texcoco into a putrid tip. This led to disease and pestilence that killed thousands of inhabitants over the following months.

The visiting kings weren't around long enough to witness this problem and after a final feast, complete with a course of hallucinogenic mushrooms, they were given rich gifts and escorted back to their domains. The Mexica had achieved their aims, consecrating the Templo Mayor, and overawed their vassals, allies, and even their enemies. No state would be likely to go to war with Ahuizotl when the consequences of defeat had been made so abundantly clear.

These gruesome cults did not survive for long. Just a few decades later, the empire which had grown so quickly, nurtured by an ever-increasing torrent of blood, was brought down by a tiny organism which the Spanish conquistadors under Hernán Cortés (1485–1547) brought with them. More deadly than the best Toledo steel or the mightiest Andalusian steed, smallpox swept through the population of Mesoamerica, sparing neither the Aztecs nor the peoples allied to the conquistadors, as a mighty empire was brought to its knees in just three years of war and plague.

HUMAN SACRIFICE

Many cultures have engaged in human sacrifice throughout history. The Scythians dwelled on the Eurasian Steppes and were one of the first societies to domesticate the horse. In the first millennium BCE, the tribes dominated their vast lands and even posed a challenge to Alexander the Great. Herodotus wrote how the tribes sacrificed humans to the god of war. Prisoners of war would be chosen, one man out of a hundred, and taken to the top of a wooden altar where wine would be poured over the victim's head from a golden chalice before their throat was cut and their blood gathered in the same golden chalice. This blood was then poured over a holy sword. At the same time the right arms of the victims were hacked off, thrown into the air, and left where they fell.

Herodotus has been called the "Father of Lies," but what he wrote about human sacrifice taking place at the burial of Scythian kings has been supported by some archaeological findings. The king was first buried within a large mound along with his concubines and steward, who were all strangled. A year later 50 of the tribe's best warriors were strangled and gutted along with their favorite horses. Man and horse were then stuffed with chaff and straw before being mounted upon wooden stakes, which were thrust through their bodies to give the illusion that the warriors were riding in a great circle around the chief's tomb.

The Incas (1438–1533) sacrificed young women after plying them with hallucinogenic drugs. Their corpses were then entombed in rocky cairns at the borders of the Inca kingdom, where it is supposed they were guardians against evil spirits entering the realm.

In Europe (around 2000 BCE—400 CE), each year a young man was given the privilege of wedding the local earth deity. For a year he ate the best foods and lived a life of leisure. Before spring he would be sacrificed by being bludgeoned and having his throat cut, then was buried in a bog to live with his "bride" forevermore.

ΗΡΟΔΟΤΟΣ

RIGHT Herodotus (484–25 BCE) is seen as the 'Father of History'. He pioneered the use of a range of evidence to form historical conclusions.

EUROPEAN BOG PEOPLE

Not as spectacular as the Aztecs, but equally gruesome, was the fate of countless Northern Europeans sacrificed to nature gods throughout Scandinavia and Europe. At least these unfortunates were given a meal of cakes or gruel before their violent end. Iron Age cult members believed that by using multiple methods of execution, they would satisfy several gods. The greater the pain, the greater the gain. Victims were garroted and stabbed, had their nipples cut off, were beaten so that their ribs cracked, were hit over the head with axes, and finally were submerged in a bog, where they were destined to spend eternity. To make sure they could not return, these gifts to the gods were pinned into their last resting places with long withies and stakes, or else had large rocks placed over their torsos.

Roman writers such as Tacitus wrote of the sacrifices the "barbarians" of the north carried out and described how they were invariably killed to satisfy nature gods to ensure good harvests. The remarkable preservative qualities of northern bogs and marshes has allowed us to understand exactly how these nature cults sent their offerings into the next world. The best preserved of these ancient "bog bodies" still seem to wail down through the ages with their contorted visages.

Lindow Man

On August 1, 1984, the remains of an Iron Age human sacrifice were unearthed in a swamp called Lindow Moss in Cheshire, England. He was immediately named Lindow Man.

In common with most human sacrifices from the period, he had been well treated before his brutal death. Examination proved that he was probably from the upper class as he appeared to be in good health and had soft, uncalloused hands, proving he was not from a farming background. His age was estimated at 25 and he was approximately 1.7 m tall.

There was evidence that he had been to the Iron Age equivalent of a day-spa just before being killed. His hair, moustache, and beard had been recently trimmed and he had even had a manicure. What was most remarkable was that he had recently consumed a meal of various grains baked into a cake. Many of the meals eaten by these sacrificial victims were made of grains and flours only available in the dead of winter. This perhaps hints at the role these individuals had to play. The timing of the sacrifice in winter suggests that they were offered to gods who were believed to rotate the earth and bring the spring and summer season.

RIGHT **Lindow Man suffered a painful death at the hands of his fellow tribesmen. He may have been killed in a ritualistic manner to facilitate good harvests.**

As the preserved corpse emerged from the bog, some injuries were immediately obvious. The scalp had two clear wounds, and

below those were two large breaks in the skull made from the same blunt instrument that had driven bone fragments into the brain. There also appeared to be cut marks just above the navel and on the right collar bone. One of his ribs had been snapped. Two vertebrae had been broken and it appeared that as one of the killers was strangling the victim another had beaten him with a heavy blow to the head or else dragged the head forward, leading to the broken neck.

On further investigation it was possible to estimate the sequence of events and manner of Lindow Man's death. He died between 2 BCE and 119 CE. He met an elaborately staged death. It is likely that first he was struck twice on top of the head with a heavy object, most likely a narrow-bladed ax. He then received a blow on the back, maybe from somebody's knee, which broke a rib and probably caused internal injuries. A thin cord placed around his throat strangled him and broke his neck, before he had his throat cut and was placed face down in a pool in the bog.

Grauballe Man

BELOW Like many of the bodies found in similar circumstances, Grauballe Man's hair turned red from immersion in the bog. Many cultures saw red hair as a sign of divinity.

Grauballe Man was discovered by peat cutters in 1952, near the town of Grauballe, Denmark. As the body emerged, despite some slippage of skin off the skull, it was immediately obvious from his tortured expression that Grauballe Man had died a painful and traumatic death. The body was sent to the Moesgaard Museum in Aarhus for examination and preservation. It soon became clear that

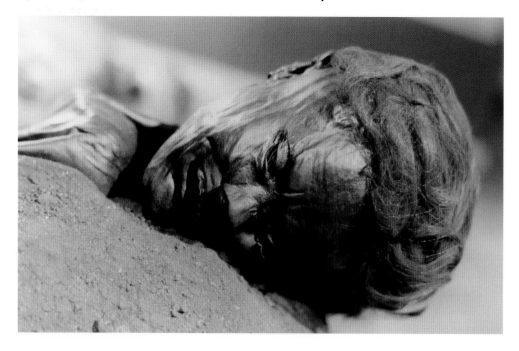

the unfortunate individual had died violently, his throat cut by a sharp weapon. The actual manner of his death was by having his neck cut open, ear to ear, severing his trachea and also his esophagus. The wound was so deep that the gullet was completely severed. It would have required several strokes by the killer. He was around 30 years old when he died. There were also skull injuries and other fractures, indicating a trifecta of deadly attacks, and it is possible that he was knocked unconscious before having his throat cut. Visual examination of his exceptionally well-preserved hands and fingers showed, in common with many other presumed sacrificial victims, no signs of manual labor.

ABOVE Grauballe Man's hand showed that he was pampered. It is possible he knew from an early age that he was to be a sacrificial offering.

Like Lindow Man, Grauballe Man is likely to have died in early spring. It is estimated that he lived sometime between 30 CE and 400 CE. An examination of his stomach revealed that Grauballe Man's last meal consisted of porridge made from corn, rye, and seeds from over 60 different herbs and grasses. These included clover, spelt rye, Yorkshire fog, rye-grass, goosefoot, buttercup, lady's mantle, black nightshade, yarrow, wild chamomile, and smooth hawksbeard. No traces of summer or autumn fruits common at the time such as strawberries, blackberries, apples, hips, or raspberries and no leafy greens were present, proving that he died before any plants had come into leaf. This indicates that he was killed at the time of midwinter celebrations, the purpose of which was to hasten the coming of spring. It was on this type of occasion where bloody human sacrifices reached a peak in the Iron Age.

THE ASSASSINS OF ALAMUT

The schism between the two competing arms of the Islamic faith, the majority Sunni and minority Shia, goes back to the century after the founding of the first Muslim state under Muhammad (571–632). From each of the two main branches various sects have grown, and it is one of the Shiite sects that has given us the word for a particularly ruthless kind of killer.

The Assassins of Alamut, as the sect was known, were in many ways the forbears of modern-day terrorist death cults, who are so single-minded in their determination to murder and maim, they think nothing of dying along with their victims. Within this 12th-century cult, young men were groomed with the promise of a wonderful afterlife if they sacrificed their earthly lives to kill the political and spiritual enemies of the leader of their sect, who

BELOW **Alamut in Iran was protected by its formidable natural defenses—a cordon of fanatical killers also ensured that none would ever try to attack the castle.**

became popularly known as the Old Man of the Mountain. Captured Assassins would grin and bear the most horrific tortures before being executed. Waiting for them was a land where wine and honey flowed like water, where gorgeous nymphets satisfied their every sexual whim, a land full of bountiful fruit trees and vines, in contrast to the harsh lands of much of the Middle East.

So deep was the conditioning that men would spend most of their adult life as "sleepers," establishing careers and families while waiting, sometimes for decades, for orders to emerge from their cover and pounce upon a target.

Teacher and Self-Proclaimed Prophet

Hassan-i Sabbah (1034–1124) was a member of the Isma'ilis, a particularly violent group within the Shiite minority. As a powerful administrator with the Persian Shah he managed to embezzle a fortune from the prince's coffers and it was this with which he built his new cult. He took his fortune and some dedicated followers and purchased the mountain fastness of Alamut castle.

Myths and legends surround the origins of the cult. It was founded in approximately 1090 and lasted until 1256 when the last strongholds were eliminated by the Mongols. Most of what we know today was written by enemies of the Assassins and these writings tend to focus on the cult's savage nature and disregard its many positives aspects.

Large areas of waste land were brought back into cultivation through massive irrigation projects. The land at the valley floor was arable, allowing for the cultivation of dry crops including barley, wheat, and rice. In order to make available the maximum amount of cultivable land, the ground was terraced under Hassan's direction. The sloping valley was broken up into step-like platforms upon which abundant food could be cultivated. In times of need the surrounding villages were well equipped to furnish the castle with ample supplies.

A tremendous library was built up which included a diverse range of writings such as Nestorian Christian tracts as well as rare classical works; alas, these were destroyed by the Mongols as they ravaged the land, determined to root out the lethal cult of vipers in their midst. The construction of Alamut's famous library likely occurred after Hasan's fortification of the castle and its surrounding valley. With its astronomical instruments and rare collection of works, the library attracted scholars and scientists from around the world, and a variety of religious persuasions, who visited it for many months at a time as guests of the Assassins.

Not averse to self-promotion, Hassan proclaimed that he had been given magical powers by the prophet himself. Additionally, a dodgy family tree was drawn up, placing his own descendants firmly within Muhammad's line. A group of fanatical loyalists was attracted to the charismatic preacher and with the funds embezzled from the Persian court he set himself up among the lofty heights of the Alborz Mountains of Iran. Hassan purchased a fortification from its owner and renamed it Alamut (Eagle's Nest). Perched on top of an inaccessible mountain deep in the high ranges to the north of Tehran, this fortification proved almost impossible to capture. Being approachable only by a precipitous pass made it easy to defend; it was said that a single archer could hold any number of men at bay given a ready supply of arrows and a sure eye. But while this mountain stronghold provided a perfect physical defense, equally efficient was the psychological terror inspired by the fanatical Fida'yin, the young men trained to seek out and destroy any target who had earned the ire of their leader.

One common story told of their devotion details how a prince was boasting to Hassan about the size of his army and the strength of his arms. Hassan responded contemptuously and explained that he did not need many fighters as they were all totally obedient. At this he instructed one of his followers to throw himself off a fortification wall. The Assassin immediately followed orders and plunged to his death on the rocks below.

The Garden of Earthly Delights

Many myths surround the methods by which these young men were made into fanatical fighters who would cast their lives away without fear. But it is likely that those attracted to the cult would have been ripe for indoctrination. Fleeing centuries of persecution and with stories of horrific revenges carried out by the Sunni majority throughout the Middle East, young Shiite men would be recruited into the sect and have their minds molded, with Hassan choosing only those he thought would become efficient killers. Some were purchased from their parents at a young age, malleable youths ripe for conditioning and brainwashing.

The most commonly told story is of how Hassan transformed a secluded corner of his domain into a walled garden out of Alamut's view. By diverting several streams through these walled pleasure palaces, a garden of earthly delights was created. Full of pomegranate and date palms as well as fragrant vines, the fountain-filled gardens were adorned with beautiful young women well skilled in the arts of lovemaking.

MANY MYTHS SURROUND THE METHODS BY WHICH THESE YOUNG MEN WERE MADE INTO FANATICAL FIGHTERS WHO WOULD CAST THEIR LIVES AWAY WITHOUT FEAR. BUT IT IS LIKELY THAT THOSE ATTRACTED TO THE CULT WOULD HAVE BEEN RIPE FOR INDOCTRINATION.

Like much that has been written about the Assassins, this is probably a mixture of fantasy and fact. It is certainly the case that huge irrigation projects created pockets of lush farmland in an otherwise desolate landscape. Access to the pleasure gardens was only possible through a secret subterranean passage from the fortress, and only when a recruit had gone through several levels of indoctrination was he taken there. Those who resisted the logic of the Assassins would be sent packing, if they were lucky, and only those who renounced their past ties in full could progress through the training to the ultimate destination. It was these chosen few, who discarded their personality, who would be admitted into the pleasure gardens of Alamut.

ABOVE A European view of the Old Man of the Mountain. Here, he issues orders to his followers while "houris" wait in the pleasure gardens.

Rendered unconscious with hashish (the Assassins were known in Arabic as the *Hashashin*) and other drugs, they would be transported through the bowels of Alamut into the pleasure gardens, and there awoken when vinegar was splashed onto their faces. Then the no doubt virginal young men would be given a taste of the afterlife promised to them. As the houris, or heavenly maidens, pleasured the

Fida'yin, they would whisper in their ears that they should hurry and die so they could return to paradise for eternity. This was only a sample, they whispered, a taste of what is waiting for the young men in the afterlife.

The maidens weren't the only trick up Hassan's sleeve. He had a deep pit dug in the floor of his chambers and buried a young acolyte therein. With only the young man's head showing, what appeared to be a plate (but in fact had a hole in the center) was placed around his neck and filled with sheep's blood. To an observer it looked like a decapitated head lay on the floor. But the head could speak and explained to the young recruits who saw it how he had followed the master's orders and found himself in paradise, no doubt dwelling on the lushness

BELOW At the peak of their powers, the Assassins had strongholds in Iran, Iraq, and Syria. This is Masyaf Castle, one of their fortifications in Syria.

of the pomegranates. Obviously this subterfuge could not be revealed and it was necessary that the young man was later properly decapitated and his head displayed on Alamut's parapets.

Having been deprived of luxuries and comforts all their lives, the young men would willingly swallow the tale they were told and pledge unswerving loyalty to their lord. Whether they really thought they had been transported to the afterlife was beside the point. Generations of oppression had primed the young recruits with the motivation to become lethal killing machines.

The Assassins utilized many of the methods used by modern-day cults. These included devotion to a charismatic leader who seemed to offer simple answers to all of life's problems, a lengthy process of indoctrination and thought reform, and economic and sexual rewards for pursuing the wishes of the cult.

As with all cults there was a strict hierarchical structure through which adherents had to pass to gain status within the organization. Sitting at the top were Hassan and his descendants. Defined within the cult as the Grand Master of the Order and known in popular culture as the Old Man of the Mountain, it was Hassan's responsibility to vet recruits, send out orders and conduct foreign policy. Hassan and his successors maintained cordial relations with neighboring rulers, one way of avoiding a dagger in the back being payment of generous subsidies to Alamut. Below the Grand Master were his trusted advisers, known as the Propagandists. Next were the Rafiqs (Companions), and lastly the Lasiqs (Adherents). It was from this last group that the Fida'yin (meaning Self-Sacrificing Agents) were selected.

Smiling Assassins

Some youths were too keen on the afterlife. Initially some committed suicide and Hassan had to modify his message and explain that only those who followed his orders could attain paradise. Most recruits were aged between 12 and 20. As well as ideological indoctrination, they were trained in the fine arts of assassination, with poison, knives, daggers, and swords the main weapons. Bows and javelins were not considered appropriate as it was important the trainee killers were able to get up close and personal with their enemy, and missile weapons would allow their targets to flee. The most common weapon was a short-bladed curved dagger. This could be easily concealed in the folds of robes and was particularly suited for the close-in work of the Assassins. Most surviving accounts of successful assassinations agree on several points. The Assassins usually attacked in groups of two to five and positioned themselves so that they came from several directions at once in an explosive surprise attack. They rained multiple blows upon their target, much like a modern-day prisoner might be attacked by knife-wielding thugs in prison. These blitz-like attacks led to multiple wounds that, while not too deep, would inflict horrendous, mortal injuries.

KILLERS WERE DISPATCHED TO TOWNS AND CITIES HUNDREDS OF MILES AWAY AND GIVEN FINANCIAL SUPPORT TO HELP THEM MELT INTO THE COMMUNITY. SOME SAW OUT THEIR DAYS IN THESE FAR-FLUNG PLACES, BUT OTHERS WERE CONTACTED BY AN ENVOY AND GIVEN A TARGET. EMERGING FROM THE CROWD, THE EMBEDDED ASSASSIN WOULD STRIKE. LOOKING FORWARD TO THE PROMISED AFTERLIFE, THEY BECAME THE ORIGINAL "SMILING ASSASSINS."

Tricks of stealth and cunning, and even foreign languages, were taught, which in the round meant the ability to blend in with their surroundings and become one with local populations throughout the Middle East. Funded from the wealth of the sect, individual Assassins could spend decades as sleepers in royal courts throughout the Muslim and Christian worlds. Rising to positions of influence or just living as humble craftsmen, no ruler, imam, or wealthy merchant could be sure that even their most trusted subordinates were not members of the deadly cult.

Although the cult initially had only one stronghold, over the following decades more and more fortifications were populated with the Assassins until a network extended throughout much of Iran and Iraq. Issuing from these inaccessible forts, a stream of trained killers emerged to terrorize populations over a period of a century and a half.

The mere whisper that an individual had offended the sect would lead to them fleeing into exile and abandoning their kith and kin. Officials being carried in a litter might find one of the bearers turned and attacked them with a knife. The governor of Homs was warned that he was a target and surrounded himself with armed guards. He dismissed them upon entering the mosque thinking that not even an Assassin would strike in such a sacred location. Wrong. Mid-prayer he was set upon by a group of knife-wielding attackers who cut him to ribbons.

Christians were fair game if the sect was paid enough. The Marquis Corrado di Montefeltro (13th century) was dining with the Bishop of Tyre. Two Assassins posing as monks launched themselves upon him, but only one managed to inflict a slight wound before being cut down. The other fled into the Bishop's chapel and hid behind the altar. As the marquis came to pray for forgiveness the remaining Assassin emerged and finished the job. Tortured by the Christian guards the Assassin went to his death with a blessed smile on his lips as he anticipated the paradise that awaited him.

Sometimes Assassins would not kill. Many a ruler was persuaded to change their policies when they woke up with a blade firmly planted in their pillow. Nizam al-Mulk (1018–92) decided to avenge the death of his son and marched with a mighty

host on Alamut. Drawing up his siege engines the emir looked forward to wiping the deadly sect from the face of the earth. When he awoke there was a glistening dagger buried up to its hilt in the sand next to his head. A note was attached, warning of his and his army's impending deaths. Whether it was one of his own men or an emissary from the heights who had left the message in the dead of night was never established. Nizam al-Mulk wisely chose to withdraw.

ABOVE Many tried to capture Alamut, including the Seljuk Turks depicted in this miniature. Only the Mongols under Hulagu Khan succeeded in 1256.

Perhaps prompting his hasty withdrawal was the knowledge that once the Assassin leadership had announced that they were going to kill a target, they would stop at nothing to achieve that aim. One or two strikes might go awry, but eventually a dedicated killer would find his way through a target's defenses and carry out his master's wishes. In this regard, Hassan and his successors were true innovators, perfecting the idea of sleeper cells or dormant operatives. Killers were dispatched to towns and cities hundreds of miles away and given financial support to help them melt into the community. Some saw out their days in these far-flung places, but others were contacted by an envoy and given a target. Emerging from the crowd, the embedded assassin would strike. Looking forward to the promised afterlife, they became the original "smiling assassins."

Seljuk Muslim rulers who targeted the Shiite minority, and the Isma'ilis in particular, were the main targets of the killing directives. The Assassins made sure that only the targeted individual was killed. Bystanders and innocent witnesses were not to be harmed, but the killers were instructed to carry out the slayings in public whenever possible. This allowed them to cultivate their terrifying reputation while not alienating the general populace. They would also not commit suicide if caught, believing this barred them from paradise.

Usually, when charged with a target, they approached their victims in disguise. While in friendly territory they favored a white tunic with a red sash, symbolizing innocence and blood.

The dynasty of ruthless Assassins was brought to a close by the remorseless attacks of the Mongol Empire. Unused to defeat and with a proud record of siege warfare, the Mongols led by Hulagu Khan (1218–65) would not allow any rival to his power to exist in the newly conquered khanate. His veteran soldiers drawn from all corners of the Mongol empire began methodically to attack each of the mountain strongholds. Trickery, brutality, and technology saw them fall one by one and their inhabitants massacred. Castles were destroyed and the fertile fields of surrounding villages laid waste.

In December 1256, even Alamut fell. A few works were salvaged from the library as well as some astronomical instruments. All else was burned to the ground and the terraced fields destroyed. Hulagu employed the Mongols' favorite tactic of scorched earth to ensure no resistance would return; any defiance was ruthlessly punished.

A few desperate adherents escaped to India where they became known as the Khojas (honorable converts), while a few tiny splinter groups remained in Iraq, Iran, and Syria. Without the financial resources of Alamut, and with their invincible reputation destroyed, the Assassins were no longer able to play a role in political affairs.

Only their legend and a deadly new profession remained.

Origins of the Name "Assassins"

The origin of the name "Assassins" is clouded in confusion. The few texts extant from Alamut, the sect's mountain seat, tell us that Hassan-i Sabbah called his disciples Asasiyun, or people faithful to the Asās, or foundation, of the faith. This could be the word misunderstood by foreign travelers, given its similarity to the word "hashish."

That is one interpretation. The first time the term appears in the historical record was when the Fatimid caliph al-Amir referred to them as hashish, a derogatory term employed to condemn those in society who were drug addicts and lived in squalor.

Anti-Shiite or anti-Isma'ili writers soon adopted the term as one of abuse. They also referred to cult members by the disparaging term Hashishiyun, meaning hashish smokers. It was taken up by Christian Crusaders, unaware of its real meaning, who took it back to Europe. Its origins forgotten, the word attained its modern English form, assassin, which in fact reflects the original activity pretty well.

LEFT A 19th-century engraving of Hassan-i Sabbah. The Assassins are renowned for the terror they inspired, but in fact Alamut was a seat of learning.

THE THUGS

ABOVE The goddess Kali is the Hindu deity of death and destruction. The Thuggee killed thousands of travelers in her name.

The Thuggee were an ancient sect that haunted the roads and waterways of the Indian subcontinent, murdering innocent travelers and merchants. No members of Indian society were safe. The poorest beggars and the richest merchants were ruthlessly killed so that the Thug gangs could seize their possessions. Whether the victim had a few bronze coins or fabulous silks and jewels, they were all fair game to be strangled by a Thug.

Like many cults they used the worship of a god as an excuse to carry out unspeakable crimes while enriching themselves in the process, calling themselves, "Children of Kali—the Destroyer and Purger of Souls." Kali's appearance matches her title. The goddess of death is portrayed with demonic, staring eyes and a protruding tongue. In one of her four hands she holds a head, dripping blood from the recently severed neck, while her other hands are depicted holding lethal weapons. In many depictions her blue body is draped in a necklace made up of human heads while the demon goddess's skirt is made of bloodied limbs. In the Indian pantheon, it was Kali's task to rid the world of useless souls, and the Thuggee appointed themselves as her disciples on earth, ready to kill any who came into their clutches.

Those killed by the Thug bands experienced a horrible death. In the dead of night, the band's leader would give a signal and his crew would leap into action. As in all cults each member had a clearly defined role. The Shumsheas (holders of hands) would leap on the victim, pinning his arms and legs to the ground, while the Bhuttote (assassin) would whip off his own rhumal (scarf) and, using a small weight sewn into its end, wrap it around the target's neck and slowly asphyxiate him. Many pictures of the Thugs carrying out their deadly trade show the victim's eyes protruding and almost bursting from their sockets as they are choked to death.

Worse was to follow. If a Thug band was to continue its deadly profession, it was imperative that the corpses sacrificed to Kali should not be found. Specialists within the group called Lughaees and Belha were tasked with disposing of the remains. As soon as the innocent travelers had been stripped of clothes, jewelry, and armor, their bodies were whisked away and buried in purpose-built pits or hiding places. It was the role of the Belha to prepare these sites. Holes dug in dry creek beds were commonly used, as were pits dug in lonely clearings in the jungle. There are instances where pits were dug under Thuggee tents, which were quickly filled in, while the Thugs continued to live above the corpses of their victims. This allayed any suspicion for other travelers.

However, the heat of the subcontinent meant that bodies soon became swollen as they putrefied in the earth, and to avoid this the Lughaees would slit the bellies of the corpses, gouge out their eyes, break all of the limbs, and slash the skin covering the main joints. These measures ensured that gases escaped the rotting cadavers and sped up the decomposition process. The Lughaees then used prepared stakes to pin the corpses deep in the earth before covering the graves with

BELOW **At a given signal the Thugs would pounce upon their target. Only the most respected members of the troupe were allowed to strangle the victim.**

scrub and stones. Many years of practice ensured that the graves were expertly camouflaged and fitted perfectly with the surrounding environment. If the gang was in a hurry these unfortunate bodies could be tossed in one of the thousands of dried wells that are still abundant all over India.

100 Percent Success Rate

The number of victims that fell prey to this cult before they were eliminated by the British colonial government was immense. While the English were interrogating cult members, horrendous confessions were made. One Bhuttote admitted to 946 murders during his 40-year career, and one band composed of only 20 Thugs was revealed to have been involved in 5,200 murders. So why were they able to get away with so much mayhem and murder from the 16th to the 19th centuries?

One of the main reasons was the secretive nature of the cult. Drawing from all sectors of Indian society, Thug bands could consist of Hindus, Muslims, higher caste, and lower. For most of the year they lived as normal people, running businesses and raising crops. Posing as respected members in the community, it appears their murderous activities were unknown even to their wives.

BELOW **A Thuggee encampment in the 1850s. All levels of Indian society were represented in the wandering bands of killers.**

But once traveling season came, the cooler months of the year on the subcontinent, they would be summoned from their lairs, using a secret language known only to the brotherhood, and sworn into a Thuggee gang. The Jemadar was the leader of the gang, responsible for nominating the meeting place and choosing his personnel. A successful Jemadar could attract hundreds to his gang. Before the band set out they were sworn to secrecy and warned that any lapse in security would be met with the direst consequences. Once the appropriate sacrifices to Kali had been made and realistic cover stories given, to account for the journey to family and friends, the band set out and began hunting humans.

Of course, secrecy is all very well, but not much use if you're careless and give yourself away, and here perhaps is the sinister reason why the Thuggee were able to operate so successfully for so long, as none who fell into their clutches ever survived. The Thugs had a 100 percent success rate, with no target ever having been known to have lived to tell of the murderous gangs.

This success rate was no doubt due to the sophisticated methods used by the roving bands of killers. Rather than traveling in a large group, the gang often spread out for many miles, moving in small unthreatening parties, communicating by subtle hand gestures or leaving signs known only to the cult.

Preceding them were the scouts, whose role was crucial to the band's success. They would infiltrate towns and find out which merchants were traveling where or when they were leaving. They would also scout out an appropriate location where the Thugs could carry out their murderous business and, most importantly, dispose of the corpses. Once the scouts had found suitable victims, they would inform the "inveiglers," whose role it was to insinuate themselves into the target's party, gaining their trust and setting them up for the kill.

Once the victim had been lulled into a false sense of security, the Thug band would congregate around the murder site, moving into positon so that all of the intended victims were surrounded by at least five Thuggee. In the dead of night, as all were relaxing around their campfires, the Jemadar gave the signal to pounce. This was often an innocuous statement such as "Bring me my tobacco." All at once the travelers were leapt upon by the band, pinned to the ground and strangled. In the blink of an eye they would be stripped of their clothes and buried in the already prepared graves.

The British estimated some 200 bands were roaming India in the 18th and 19th centuries, ranging from as few as five members to large groups numbering in the hundreds. During their murderous existence, spanning many centuries, millions of innocent Indians must have died at their hands.

As a sign of their disgrace, captive Thugs would be manhandled by the untouchables, the Mang, the lowest of the low within the Indian caste system. These

River Thugs

A unique subset of these murderous gangs, the River Thugs, was found on the River Ganges, the Hindus' sacred river. Estimated to number 300, they made a specialty of luring pilgrims onto their well-appointed boats on the river. The River Thugs also used the rhumal and were given different roles within the gang. The key difference was that these murderers didn't need to bury their victims but would haul them overboard to join the many carcasses already flowing in the divine waters, particularly those half-burned bodies where an impoverished family did not have the resources to properly immolate their deceased relatives on a funeral pyre before throwing them into the sacred waters. The other key difference was the timing of the deaths. Once the bunij (target) had been lured onto the boat, the vessel would chart a course to the middle of the river and, at the signal of three taps on the deck, the Thugs would pounce upon their victim and murder him. The corpse then had its back broken by being bent backward until the spine snapped, whereupon the luckless traveler was tossed into the water.

RIGHT The river Ganges was the scene of horrific murders carried out by the River Thugs.

impure and unwashed creatures would bind the arms of the Thug and drag him to an execution tree beyond the city walls. The tied-up Thug would be thrown face down on the ground, and one of the untouchables would take a machete and hack both legs of the condemned just above the heel, severing the Achilles tendons. A noose would then go around the neck, and with his arms pinioned and unable to lift his legs, the Thug would slowly asphyxiate as he was hauled up to hang from the tree. This was in fact a merciful punishment. If the local nawab wanted to make an example of a captured Thug, he could condemn him to a living hell. Firstly, his nose would be sliced off, and the skin drawn over the gaping wound and crudely sewn together to make a horrific mess of the once proud visage. Then the Thug would have his hands chopped off before the stumps were dipped in boiling pitch to cauterize the wounds. Or else the Thug would have his cheeks and forehead branded with the Hindu letters for Thug, making sure he could never deceive innocent travelers again. Thugs captured by the British often had the word tattooed on their cheeks just under the eyes.

Some Thugs were chained to the foreleg of an elephant. The mahout, the elephant's keeper, would make the animal break into a run, and the Thug usually lasted a maximum of two steps before he was pounded into jelly. One specialty adopted by the British from the local rulers was to tie the criminals over the mouth of a cannon, facing down the barrel, before blowing them to kingdom come with round shot through the guts. The gunners and onlookers were invariably showered with body parts in these gruesome displays, and a point was surely made.

ABOVE **Noor Khan, a "Mussulman Thug." In an instant he could convert his head dress into a lethal rhumal (strangling scarf) and dispatch his victim.**

Targeted by the British

While these punishments were horrible to behold, they were fairly rare and few Thugs had their murderous careers terminated in this manner. It wasn't until the British conquered much of the subcontinent that the Thugs at last faced a genuine challenge to their continued existence.

The first time they came to the attention of the British was in the district of Etawah in 1808. The Thugs operating in this area were obviously overconfident and did not dispose of their victims in the correct manner. Thomas Perry was the East India Company's magistrate in the region, a role that involved soldiering, policing, and taxation, which he took up in 1811. Hundreds of bodies were being retrieved from ditches and wells along the major roads, all strangled and mutilated in the same way before being tossed into any convenient place without any attempt at concealment. From one well alone, 15 cadavers were retrieved. Unsure what was happening the magistrate increased police patrols and posted a 1,000-rupee reward for any information regarding the murders. Finally, after 18 months a suspicious group was arrested after a local man's tip-off, and under interrogation a young Kyboola, or novice Thug, admitted what he was.

The Thug's name was Gholam Hossyn, and he and some of the band he was arrested with were willing to reveal a great deal about the gang's methods when under further interrogation by Perry. The method of using the rhumal was demonstrated to a horrified court and the young man displayed his proficiency at turning an innocent piece of cloth into a garrotte by tying a knot at the end of the scarf and whipping the cloth around the subject's throat. The knot stayed in the assassin's hand and was used as a kind of handle to wind the material tightly around the neck.

BELOW **Multhoo Byragee Jogee, of Ajmere, aged 90, a convicted Thug. Thugs who turned informers were given a life sentence. Their families were cared for as long as the Thugs told the truth.**

Most surprising to Perry was the description of the wide-ranging nature of the gangs. Few, he was told, operated within 200 miles of their home base, so as to avoid detection. The informants also suggested that there were up to 1,200 Thuggee living in that part of India. They told how once a murder had been committed

the group would quickly leave the scene of the crime and move into another jurisdiction before their next attack, making detection and arrest almost impossible for any authority. Much of India at this time was independent of British rule and Perry was aware how difficult it was to get local rulers to cooperate with the colonial powers. Nevertheless, through his investigations Perry was able to arrest some 70 Thugs while forcing the remainder to flee to the adjoining lands; for a period of time strangled bodies were not to be found in the province of Etawah. However, Perry was reminded just how resilient the Thuggee society was when in 1812 bodies began appearing again in wells along the roads around his station. Most of the arrested Thugs retracted their confession when brought to trial, and lacking evidence the courts were forced to acquit. Many others had returned to their homes and began again to practice their ancient skills.

ABOVE **While Thugs worshipped Kali, they kept all of their ill-gotten gains. The chief aim of their expeditions was to get rich by murdering innocent travelers.**

Despite these setbacks Perry's activities as well as several reports written by other British administrators scotched any doubt in the minds of the occupying British that Thugs were a menace that would have to be dealt with eventually. The reports also solved one other mystery which had been worrying the English military. Many sepoys (native soldiers) had been going missing when returning home on their annual leave. It became obvious that these cashed-up soldiers were perfect targets for the Thuggee, so regulations were printed urging the sepoys to avoid company on their route home and not to accept food or drink from strangers. The total sum of British knowledge on the Thugs was compiled in an influential report by Dr. Richard Sherwood entitled "Of the murderers called Phansigars," printed in 1816 and again in 1820.

Wiping Out the Thugs

It wasn't until several years later, when an ambitious Captain William Sleeman (1788–1856) decided to wipe out the Thuggee altogether, that they faced their greatest challenge. English officers remarked upon the complete absence of guilt or remorse among captured Thugs when discussing the innocent people they had murdered. The thrill of the hunt and the kill stood out, and all admitted that if they were ever free to practice their profession, they would take to it again like a fish to water. The Thugs did feel remorse, but only for a woman they lost or a particularly rich merchant who escaped their clutches. This lack of conscience must be partly attributable to the strict religious rituals that were held to honor their profession in the name of Kali.

It was this devotion and love for their trade that convinced the British that all the gangs had to be rounded up and convicted; that Thugs should never be allowed to re-enter Indian society. Sleeman had developed a great affection for the Indian people as he had risen through the ranks of the East India Company, and he saw it as his duty to eliminate the Thuggee and their murderous ways. He also noticed that other British officers who had successfully arrested and prosecuted gangs of Thugs had received positive commendations or even promotions. Sleeman desperately wanted to stand out from the pack, so he turned to his new task with a will.

Thugs were possessed of what they considered to be a strict moral code, one element of which was never to inform on one another. This obligation was reinforced not so much from a sense of guilt—as we have seen, remorse was not a moral quality much prized among them—but from the palpable threat of violence from other Thugs should they discover such treachery. Sleeman decided that to be able to crack the Thug network, he needed to get the murderers to turn on each other, and this he did with threats of death, exile, and life imprisonment.

In February 1830, Sleeman and his battalions of mounted troops arrested a gang of Thugs who had dispatched 30 victims and amassed at least 2,000 rupees in booty during their most recent expedition. The gang had fallen upon a group of sepoys, but one of the Bhuttotes missed his mark and only managed to get his rhumal over the soldier's nose rather than around his throat. The lucky sepoy put up a desperate struggle and escaped, alerting another patrol nearby. Although the band scattered, Sleeman was able to send out soldiers and the majority were arrested.

Four of the gang were turned and became approvers, Thugs who were willing to give lengthy legal depositions detailing their past activities, the sites where attacks and burials had taken place, the actions of the other members of the gang, and, most importantly, the whereabouts and actions of other Thugs in the district. The information was organized into a large deposition supported by goods found on the Thugs and statements from other witnesses. The case was successfully prosecuted and 15 members of the gang were hung while others were transported or imprisoned.

Sleeman elevated the role of approvers and made them a set above the men they informed on. He ensured that they were well fed and clothed, and to seal the deal provided a pension for the approver's family if the information provided by the Thug turncoats proved accurate. They were also spared the threat of execution and transportation. Such was the success of this scheme that they soon considered themselves to be paid employees of the British Raj. They were physically separated from their peers for their own protection.

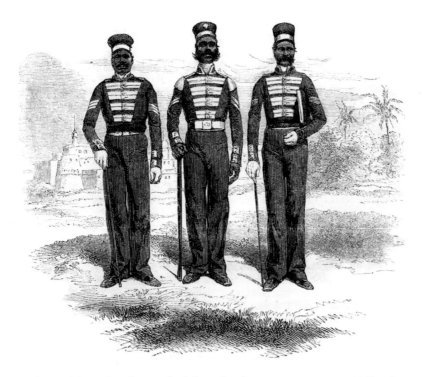

The guidelines that Sleeman laid down for the approvers were very proscriptive. Firstly, the Thug had to provide a full and frank disclosure of every crime he had been involved in and full details of all who had been associated with those crimes. This included their names, aliases, caste, and places of residence. Secondly, he had to give all aid possible to arrest and convict all guilty persons, including relatives or friends. Thirdly, any failure to satisfy either of the above would lead to an immediate cessation of protection from the death penalty and an end to any privileges for the Thug or his family.

ABOVE **Indian sepoys. Many rich merchants paid soldiers such as these to escort their valuable merchandise on the lawless roads of the subcontinent.**

Following the guidelines laid down by Sleeman, approvers throughout the British domains gave depositions supporting each other's accusations, even though they were taken hundreds of miles apart. A huge dossier was compiled which listed every known Thug, the gangs he had associated with, and the crimes they had committed. Further evidence was gathered when approvers took parties of police and sepoys to the sites of previous crimes and exhumed the bodies of those who had been killed, in some cases many years before. Sometimes relatives of missing travelers accompanied these expeditions, and although the bodies were frequently corrupted beyond all recognition, a particular sandal or item of clothing would often be recognized, allowing identification of the victim and further supporting evidence to be gathered for trial.

Chained in light irons that could easily be concealed under loose clothing, approvers often accompanied these patrols, their role to identify fellow Thugs, allowing them to be arrested. They also pointed out the identities of imprisoned Thugs. Rewards for capture of the more notorious Thugs were often paid out to the families of approvers, a strong inducement in poverty-stricken India. By the end of 1830, hundreds of arrests had been made and, thanks to the huge weight of evidence gathered, only a few suspects failed to be convicted. Over the next few years, 100 proven approvers were recruited and successful trials of thousands of Thugs took place throughout India. Intricate genealogies as well as detailed maps showing the depredations of Thugs across the subcontinent allowed the Thuggee Department to identify at least 4,000 suspected gang members.

LEFT This 1901 depiction of a Thuggee human sacrifice is inaccurate. Men, women, and children died silently as soon as they were attacked.

The soldiers tasked with tracking down suspects were motivated by revenge for their murdered peers as well as generous bounties. One patrol that hunted down a prominent Jemadar received several hundred rupees each, the equivalent of several years' wages. Once the Thugs were captured, they were detained in the centralized British judicial system rather than returned to their place of origin where bribes could easily lead to an early release. When hauled before the judge the weight of evidence accumulated by Sleeman and his men led to speedy convictions. Laws were passed in 1836 making the simple act of being recognized as a Thug, whether they had killed or not, punishable by life imprisonment with hard labor. Even those who escaped conviction could be held by the authorities until they were able to pay the huge surety demanded for their release.

Then in 1843 a law was passed giving the British authorities the legal right for any Thug held in a local jail to be seized and held in an East India Company jail for the term of their natural life. Most local rulers saw the writing on the wall and were content to cooperate with the British. By the mid 1840s, Thuggee had been pretty much eliminated throughout the subcontinent, and by 1848 a triumphant Sleeman was able to report that no incident had been reported throughout India that year.

The Thugs had been arrested, and now it was time to make them pay for their crimes. Between 1826 and 1848, 4,500 men were tried for being Thuggee and of these 504 were hanged. Three thousand were sentenced to life in prison, and all but another 25, who were found not guilty, were given other, lighter sentences.

Those who were proven to be a Jemadar, a Bhuttote, or a Shumshea were sentenced to be hanged. Most who witnessed these executions commented on the perfectly composed manner in which the condemned met their fate. Marched from the prison gate, each would calmly select his own noose and place it around his own neck. They would then allow themselves to be pinioned and, just before stepping off the blocks upon which they stood, many would yell out, "Glory to Kali! Kali's glory!"

THE BOXERS

The I Ho Ch'uan (the Righteous and Harmonious Fists—hence the name Boxers) were a crazy cult with a single aim: to kill the foreign devils who seemed intent on taking China from the Chinese during the 19th century.

Japanese, German, English, Americans, and even the Italians used their superior weaponry to force the Chinese Manchu dynasty to give generous trading concessions. To counter these hostile forces, the Boxers drew on hundreds of years of Chinese martial arts to produce supermen who would restore Chinese pride.

Boxers spent many hours performing and perfecting their martial arts skills. As well as unarmed forms, they practiced martial arts that used traditional curved halberds and spears. Incantations and spells were combined with physical exercises similar to kung fu to produce a trance-like state which made them impervious to negative emotions such as fear or doubt. Some practitioners sought to perfect the mystical "iron shirt," which involved tensing the muscles on the torso to such an extent that the practitioner became able to resist blows and even bullets.

The Boxers classified all foreigners as first-class devils, those Chinese who had converted to Christianity as second-class devils, and those who were employed by foreigners as third-class devils. All were fair game and in 1900 the Boxers sought to expel or kill any Westerners in what has become known as the Boxer Uprising. Two hundred missionaries were massacred along with 3,000 converts. The Boxers surrounded the European legations in Peking (modern-day Beijing), but soon learnt that red banners and scarves were not enough to combat modern breech-loading weaponry.

Following the rebellion thousands of Boxers were rounded up and almost invariably killed by beheading, flaying, and dismemberment. Many suffered lingchi—the infamous death by a thousand cuts.

The method of lingchi for executions had been used by Chinese governments for hundreds

BELOW The Boxers were very effective at massacring Western civilians and Chinese Christians. They were not so good at fighting Western armies.

of years. The Chinese believed that to be able to experience a pleasant afterlife it was necessary for a person to be buried as an intact body. Lingchi was reserved for the most heinous crimes as it dismembered the body, preventing a good afterlife, and inflicted horrific pain, ensuring that the last moments of the criminal's life was spent in agonized suffering. The lingchi practitioner first bound the captive before using a range of razor-sharp knives to slice off slabs of skin, nipples, facial features, and so on. The courts that sentenced criminals to lingchi were very specific as to how long the torture should last. Once the torture had been completed a sharp blade was used to pierce the heart before the lifeless body was dismembered.

BELOW **A satirical cartoon depicting foreign powers' involvement in the Boxer Rebellion.**

WEWELSBURG CASTLE

It could be argued that Himmler's SS was the ultimate killer cult. Indoctrinated with arcane pagan beliefs, the black-clad SS instigated a reign of terror throughout Europe. At the heart of their belief was the mystical nature of Wewelsburg Castle.

Few castles in Europe had such a dark past. In 1654 the triangle-shaped castle became a stronghold for the Inquisition. Thousands of suspected heretics, criminals, and witches were held prisoner, tortured, burned at the stake, or hanged at Wewelsburg before it ceased to be a prison in 1802.

Himmler added to its dark history by using labor from the nearby concentration camp. As World War Two progressed and Nazi success seemed assured, Himmler had new plans drawn up for the heart of his dark empire. Radiating out from Wewelsburg was a complex that would include training schools, uniform workshops, and museums that were intended to house relics such as the Holy Grail and the Ark of the Covenant once they were recovered. The complex would have a spiritual as well as military role. Colleges would be established to teach hypnosis, divination, and psychic mediumship. Research fellows would investigate new ways to find energy to reach the stars.

The heart of the Wewelsburg complex was the *Obergruppenführersaal* (Generals' Hall), which was a stone-lined chamber in the north tower where Himmler installed a round table in imitation of the Round Table of King Arthur. Twelve top SS generals were to meet here in the impressive arched space adorned with Nazi and Nordic symbols. Carved into the ceiling was a Swastika inside a sun wheel—a "black sun."

Wewelsburg was nicknamed "Black Camelot" by other Nazi top brass. When he could escape from his role as security supremo, Himmler returned to the castle and performed many ceremonies. These included welcoming in the winter solstice, SS weddings, initiation ceremonies, and worship of the eternal Aryan flame.

RIGHT **Wewelsburg Castle was the spiritual heart of Heinrich Himmler's SS empire.**

The Manson Family

Eighteen-year-old Steven Parent (1951–69) was in the wrong place at the wrong time. Earlier that week he had struck up a conversation with William Garretson (1950–2016), who was the caretaker of Roman Polanski's (1933–) palatial residence on 10050 Cielo Drive in the Hollywood Hills. The 19-year-old Garretson had expressed an interest in purchasing a tape recorder and on the evening of August 8, 1969 Parent had driven up into the hills to show him one.

The two young men chatted in the caretaker's bungalow at the rear of the property for a short time before Steven Parent walked around to the front and got in his Rambler for the short drive home. Parent was just about to place his key in the ignition when a tall man loomed out of the darkness. He was holding an old long-barrelled .22 pistol in one hand and a bayonet in the other. Parent had a split second to scream "No!" before he was shot four times and the bayonet slashed across his throat.

The innocent boy who wanted to sell a cassette recorder had crossed paths with a gang of murderers who roamed California leaving bloody carnage in their wake.

BELOW **The Spahn Ranch today. It was from this location that "The Family" descended to the suburbs below to carry out murder and mayhem.**

On the orders of their guru they would descend from their hardscrabble Spahn Ranch in the hills above Death Valley to kill and murder. Charles Manson (1934–) wanted to create so much mayhem that the blacks of America would rise up and kill their "superior" white fellow citizens. Only Manson's "Family" would survive, hidden away in its safe subterranean lair, and once the carnage was complete they would emerge and rule the new society through their superior intelligence and cunning.

Through a combination of LSD, sex, violence, and fear, Manson was able to convince his followers that this race war—which he referred to as Helter Skelter—was inevitable, and it was their task to speed it up with random violent attacks.

To do this he needed a high-profile murder. This was achieved on that dark night on Cielo Drive. Roman Polanski was a film director who had a habit of courting controversy. Fortunately for him, he was out of town that evening. His actress wife, Sharon Tate, who was heavily pregnant with their baby, was entertaining friends. While not a great actor, she made up for this in Polanski's eyes with her sweet nature and loving disposition. But Sharon and her friends would encounter brutality beyond their worst nightmare.

Manson was familiar with the house from a previous tenant with whom he had had business dealings, and that night had sent his gang of murderers to kill anybody they found there. Led by tall "Tex" Charles Watson (1945–), the gang had driven to the property, left their car on the road, and stealthily crept through the large grounds. Tex cut the telephone wires first. Behind Tex were several fanatical female cult members, all in their late teens and early twenties, including Susan Atkins (1948–2009), who would later boast of her role in the attacks. Having disabled the house's electrical system, the gang moved in for the kill.

Parent was the first to die, before the gang had broken into the house. Then bloody mass murder ensued. Abigail Folger (1943–69) had fled out of the front door but was hunted down and stabbed with a kitchen knife. Her boyfriend, Wojciech Frykowski (1936–69), had tried to help Abigail but was shot in the back with the .22,

THROUGH A COMBINATION OF LSD, SEX, VIOLENCE, AND FEAR, MANSON WAS ABLE TO CONVINCE HIS FOLLOWERS THAT THIS RACE WAR—WHICH HE REFERRED TO AS HELTER SKELTER—WAS INEVITABLE, AND IT WAS THEIR TASK TO SPEED IT UP WITH RANDOM VIOLENT ATTACKS.

ABOVE The victims who died at Cielo Drive. From left, Voityck Frykowski, Sharon Tate, Stephen Parent, Jay Sebring, and Abigail Folger.

pistol-whipped at least 13 times, and stabbed 51 times. The killers later reported that when they had burst into Sharon Tate's bedroom, she had looked up thinking it was a joke. She soon realized it wasn't when they dragged her into the living room and she saw the bloodied body of her former fiancé, Jay Sebring (1933–69), lying on the floor with a towel over his head. Despite screaming for mercy, especially for her unborn child, Sharon was hung from a beam over the living room floor with a rope that was also tied around Sebring's neck, and then stabbed with the bayonet at least 16 times. "Look, bitch, I have no mercy for you," was the retort to her plea.

The gang then fulfilled their master's wishes by writing "Pig" on the doors in their victims' blood. By daubing bloody words all around the horrific scene, Manson wanted to incite the police to arrest black people and thus precipitate the race war. Their work done, the killing squad sped off, only stopping a couple of times to toss

ABOVE Polanski and Tate on their wedding day. They had no connection to Manson.

away their bloodstained clothes and the murder weapons.

After several hours' driving, they got to the Manson ranch and boasted of how they had killed some "pigs." But Manson wasn't done. The next night, August 10, 1969, another murder party descended from the hills. This target was more random. Manson selected an expensive-looking house, the residence of wealthy businessman Leno LaBianca (1925–69) and his wife Rosemary (1929–69).

Their end was equally gruesome. Both were tied up and told they had nothing to fear. But then Leno was set upon and stabbed and strangled. A carving fork and knife were rammed into his stomach and a hood placed over his head. Hearing the commotion Rosemary had desperately sought to go to her husband's aid but was strangled with an electric cord on the couple's bed before being stabbed 41 times.

The crew then cut the word "WAR" into the middle-aged man's chest and on the wall of the living room wrote, "DEATH TO PIGS," and elsewhere, "HELTER SKELTER."

It seemed a reign of terror was about to descend on California. But, remarkably, the police didn't connect the two attacks. Even with the bloody writing on the wall and the violent assaults with multiple stabbings, initial inquiries were directed elsewhere. The California police proved themselves to be less than competent. The pistol used in the attack was found by a young lad and handed to the police. No connection was made until the boy's father made repeated phone calls to the hotline established by the police to solicit information. The discarded bloody clothes were only found after a crew of journalists tried to work out the perpetrators' escape route and spotted the garments where they had been tossed down an almost sheer cliff face. In fact, Susan Atkins, separately arrested on suspicion of another cult murder, confessed the crimes to her cellmate, but the police were unwilling to listen to the report.

Gradually, testimony from a number of visitors to the Spahn Ranch alerted the police to the fact that Charles Manson and his family were responsible for the murders. They were rounded up and put on trial, during the nine-month course of which a shocking story of sex, drugs, and murder held the nation spellbound.

Starting the Family

Manson, born November 12, 1934, never knew his father. As a youth he was shuffled between uninterested relatives, his alcoholic prostitute mother, and various agencies. During this time, he developed a ratlike cunning and a burning hatred for society. As a young man he was in and out of jail and developed aberrant sexual tastes including rape. Manson seemed bent on a course of petty crime until he was released from prison in 1967. He stumbled into the "turn on, tune in, drop out" culture of San Francisco. Here he found that a plentiful supply of hallucinogenic drugs and average music abilities, combined with a generic religion that seemed to pull strands from Christianity, Buddhism, and anything else that appealed, allowed him to begin his own cult.

Manson is a slight individual who, more than anything else, resembles a hairy rat. But photos don't show the power of his eyes or the force of his personality. It seems he was particularly adept at seducing lost and lonely young women, whom he would bring into his intimate circle. These women were then used as honey traps to lure males to the cult. Soon he had attracted a hardcore of fanatical devotees.

The group wandered around for a while and even stayed for a period of time in the mansion of Dennis Wilson (1944–83), the drummer of the Beach Boys. They eventually ended up with free lodgings in Spahn Ranch where the owner, old man Spahn, was kept sweet with continual sexual favors from one of the young cultists. (She tried to get him to sign a will leaving her the property, but fortunately for him he refused.) It was while in this remote ranch in Death Valley that Manson consolidated his hold on the cult members.

The cult sustained itself partly through its young women being sent out to beg or sell sexual favors. Another revenue stream was to steal Volkswagens and then convert them into dune buggies, which were then sold on. Male visitors Manson wanted to impress were

BELOW **Members of The Family in 1973. Manson kept them in line with a mixture of drugs, sex, violence, and a fear of the apocalypse.**

ABOVE Susan Atkins said "I have no mercy for you" as she stabbed Sharon Tate in the belly. She used Tate's blood to write "Pig" on a door.

offered any number of young women to make them stay, and drug-fueled orgies were common. LSD and cannabis, or pot, were common, as the group bonded with heterosexual and homosexual orgies beneath the stars or within the makeshift compound.

The settlement was nothing to rave about. Some slept in bunkers dug out of the ground and covered with corrugated iron. Others slept higgledy-piggledy in the dilapidated house. There was an old bus in the grounds which served as the cult's wardrobe. Clothes were tossed on the floor when not being worn, and anybody could grab what they wanted. This of course posed something of a challenge to the LaBianca–Tate murder investigators when looking for incriminating evidence for the murders.

Despite the squalor it seems that Manson had picked up the knack of giving his followers whatever they wanted to make them wholly subservient to his will. It

RIGHT Charles Manson after his arrest for the Tate–LaBianca murders. Some say he was most comfortable in jail and would have returned voluntarily.

THE CULT SUSTAINED ITSELF PARTLY THROUGH ITS YOUNG WOMEN BEING SENT OUT TO BEG OR SELL SEXUAL FAVORS. ANOTHER REVENUE STREAM WAS TO STEAL VOLKSWAGENS AND THEN CONVERT THEM INTO DUNE BUGGIES, WHICH WERE THEN SOLD ON.

was noticed during the subsequent murder trial that with a glance he could silence the cult members if they were making a fuss. Whatever he did his followers would instantly copy. When Manson carved a swastika in his forehead the entire cult followed suit without hesitation by heating up needles and using them to burn crosses on their heads.

It is an indication of the amount of drugs his flock was taking that they swallowed his crazy ideology hook, line, and sinker. Manson was influenced by a wide range of thinkers (in the broadest sense of the word) including Adolf Hitler (1889–1945), L. Ron Hubbard (1911–86) and the Scientologists, Christianity, the Old Testament, Buddhism, Black Magic, Hopi Indian mysticism, and even the Beatles. The *White Album* was his favorite piece of music and is where he got his key ideology, "Helter Skelter."

Helter Skelter

There were two key ideas behind Helter Skelter. Using the Book of Revelation, Manson (or "son of man," and therefore Jesus, to the Family) predicted the coming apocalypse. He placed it within the racist politics of the time and saw that the "inferior" blacks, as he saw them, would rise up and attack the whites. It was his job to provoke the attacks by killing whites in shocking crimes. Whites would witness these crimes and turn on their black servants, who would fight back and kill the whites. Muslim blacks would then engage in civil war with the remaining African American population until only a few were left alive.

All this time the Family would be sheltering in a huge bottomless cavern underground and would grow to the biblical number 144,000, as written in the Book of Revelation. The entrance to the cave was near their ranch in Death Valley, a golden cavern where there was eternal daylight. Running through its middle was a river of milk and honey, while the vast plain within the cavern was covered with mystical fruit trees that bore 12 different kinds of fruit.

According to Manson's megalomaniac fantasy, after a short time the poor blacks would be unable to run their affairs and would invite the cult to emerge from their golden cavern to rule over them as benevolent dictators. They would also become

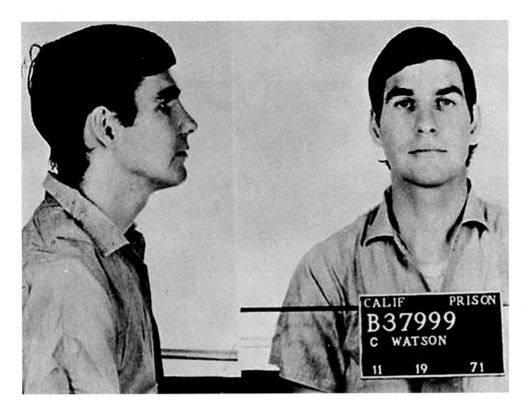

CALIF   PRISON
B37999
C WATSON
11   19   71

the whites' willing servants. Of course, Manson was the head of the cult so in real terms he was destined to become ruler of the world!

Manson decided sometime ahead of August 1969 that he would have to bring Helter Skelter about. He set about training the cult members for the murders. The first dark art they had to master was that of doing the "creepy crawl." Members were taught the basics of housebreaking and would visit houses in the middle of night, break in and do a "creepy crawl." The aim was to move around and not disturb the residents before disappearing unseen back into the gloom.

ABOVE Tex Watson was the cult's enforcer. He followed Manson's instructions to maim and kill without a second's hesitation.

He also conducted a "murder school," where the young women were given buck knives and trained how to stick "pigs." Methods practiced were slitting throats from ear to ear by grabbing the hair and pulling back the head. Or else they were to stab the victims in their ears, eyes, and guts, and wiggle the lethal long blades around so as to cause as much internal damage as possible.

Manson then went one step further and announced on the afternoon of Friday August 8th that "Now is the time for Helter Skelter." After dinner that evening he told four members, Tex (Charles Watson) and three young women—Sadie (Susan Denise Atkins, 1948-2009), Katie (Patricia Krenwinkel, 1947–), and Linda (Linda Kasabian,

1949–)—to go get a knife and a change of clothes. Linda was a recently joined and unproven member but was no doubt chosen because she had a driver's license, though as things turned out, she refused to be involved in the killings and became the prosecution's star witness once the trial began.

That night, the four piled into an old car, with Manson instructing the girls to do whatever Tex told them. He had given Tex the target address a few days earlier, and it is likely that the young man had done a reconnaissance. Three knives and a pistol wrapped in cloth were handed to Linda, who was told to throw them out if stopped by police. Manson's last instruction was to write something "witchy."

The Family hit squad proceeded to Cielo Drive. They parked at the bottom of the estate. Tex clipped the phone wires and the group scrambled over the fence. Just as they were crossing, they froze as some headlights came on. Tex told the rest to hold positions while he solved the problem.

Linda had originally been told that they were going on another "creepy crawly" mission, but she realized Manson's real intent when she heard Steven Parent pleading for his life before he was shot four times.

The group then approached the house. There were no external lights on, and Tex gained access by slitting a window screen. He then told Linda to return to the car in the driveway, from where she witnessed the bloody mayhem that followed.

The first thing she heard was a man begging for his life then screaming very loudly. A babble of terrified voices was clear in the still night. Linda then saw Sadie, Tex, and Katie pursuing two of the victims out of the house, and bludgeoning and stabbing them to death.

In a few minutes it was over. Linda panicked and ran back to the car, intending to drive off, but just as she started the ignition the three murderers appeared, covered in blood. They drove off, only stopping to discard clothes and weapons on their way back to Spahn Ranch.

Manson had dispatched the crew and he was there when it returned at 2:00 a.m. He debriefed the team, asking if they felt any remorse. He also instructed them to wash the car inside and out, and to clean themselves up. He seemed satisfied when told that the killings were messy, loud, and bloody.

The next evening Manson took a more direct role. He guided the hit squad up to the LaBianca residence and ordered the crew to wait in the car while he went inside. He "creepy-crawled" the middle-aged couple's house, this time cowing the married couple with a gun and tying them up.

Manson returned to the crew, again led by Tex, and sent them in to finish the job. When the bloody work was done, Manson drove through a predominantly black area and threw Leno's and Rosemary's wallets out the window. His aim, of course, to implicate the black community in the murders and start the race war.

Manson had clearly initiated and even been involved in these murders. In the lengthy trial that followed, the depth of his involvement and the hold he still had over the cult members became ever clearer to the jury. One of his defense attorneys earned Manson's ire and was murdered while trekking. Another witness and former cult member who was due to testify against Manson was given a burger laced with LSD. While not lethal, the high dose could easily have cost the woman her sanity if her stomach hadn't been pumped.

ABOVE **Cult members Leslie Van Houten, Patricia Krenwinkel, and Susan Atkins arrive at court to hear the formal pronouncement of their sentences.**

Manson and his fellow killers were sentenced to death but were saved by the US Supreme Court's temporary halt on the death penalty. All are still serving life sentences despite frequent requests for parole.

With the incarceration of Manson, the Family began to dwindle, with only a few diehard supporters still following his personality cult. Nevertheless, the full story of this killer cult may remain forever untold. Manson himself claims to be responsible for 38 deaths, and there are no doubt many crimes associated with him that we still do not know about.

CHAPTER 4

ANCIENT ORDERS

THE APPEAL OF SECRET SOCIETIES SEEMS to be ingrained in our DNA. Even now hunter-gatherer societies have mysterious ceremonies that only selected members of a clan are allowed to attend. Secret knowledge and elaborate initiations are characteristic of these and other modern secret societies. The Knights Templar and the Holy Vehm were violent secret societies that, even after the passage of hundreds of years, remain inscrutable and mysterious. For centuries the Masons were a mysterious brotherhood, and only now are their complex rituals emerging.

THE SPANISH INQUISITION

The Inquisition had long been a tool used by the Catholic Church to hunt down heretics. In both France and Spain this shadowy organization collected information from informers and carried out torture in dark, hidden places. Although inquisitors appeared in public for the ritual executions of Protestants, Cathars, Jews, and Muslims, most of the time they were a secretive organization that hid their methods and dossiers from the public gaze. Many of the Inquisition's personnel wore masks when on duty. They removed them while mixing with the community, making sure the public never knew who was watching them and never knew who the spies were in their midst.

The French Inquisition pioneered secretive methods of infiltrating subversive Cathar organizations during the Albigensian Crusades (1209–29). But it was when Queen Isabella and King Ferdinand of Spain established the Spanish Inquisition (1478)

BELOW **Tomas de Torquemada, Grand Inquisitor of the Spanish Inquisition, exhorts King Ferdinand II and Queen Isabella to punish all Spanish heretics.**

under Tomás de Torquemada (1420–98) that the Inquisition became a secret society which established a reputation for terror that echoes down the centuries. Indeed, many of the secretive techniques developed by Torquemada are still used by repressive regimes today.

There were more than 140,000 Jews throughout Spain and many more *conversos*, entire communities of Christians who had converted from Judaism centuries earlier. The *conversos* were mistrusted by many Spanish, who believed they still carried out Jewish rituals in secret. It was the Spanish Inquisition's task to root them out.

The name "Torquemada" struck fear into hundreds of thousands of innocent minds. *Torque* is from the Latin verb for "to twist" and *quemada* means "burned" in Spanish, thus evoking what had been the preferred method of destroying heretics for hundreds of years, making it the perfect *nom de guerre* for the Grand Inquisitor. According to those ancient practices, a garrote would twist the life out of those who confessed,

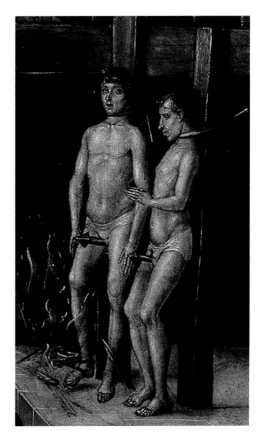

ABOVE **Those who confessed to heretical practices would be strangled with a garrote before they were burned to death.**

but those who did not renounce heresy would die by being burned at the stake. Torquemada would continue this tradition.

Once appointed to the coveted role, Tomás set about creating a secretive police state like no other. At the heart of the structure were his "Instructions." They codified exactly what was required of a good inquisitor, and armed with their strictures his ruthless subordinates spread throughout the Spanish Empire torturing and burning their way through the population.

Firstly, a good inquisitor had to keep perfect records. A suspect's family, his connections, and his history were all recorded in minute detail. Most importantly, the inquisitor had to list all of the assets the subject possessed. If found guilty of heresy, all of these were transferred to the crown.

When an inquisitor moved into a new town to "cleanse" it of heresy, he brought a fearsome retinue of *alguacils*—the inquisitorial police. These notorious torturers often wore hoods to conceal their identity, adding to the feeling of terror experienced by the community.

LEFT **Torquemada was a cold individual. He lived a life of abstinence and had one pleasure in life—torturing and burning any who were not true Catholics.**

The chief aim of the inquisitor was to track down *conversos* who had slipped back into their old Jewish ways. Torquemada's Instructions gave advice on how to identify these heretics. Neighbor was encouraged to inform upon neighbor, and even the smallest Jewish observance would result in arrest. Thousands found themselves locked away in the terrifying Inquisition dungeons. Their only contact with the world beyond their cell was when the hooded and masked *alguacils* hauled them up for interrogation.

Article 15 of Torquemada's Instructions allowed for torture to be administered if heresy was "half-proven." This catch-all statement allows even the smallest suspicion to be elevated to the status of proof. This allowed "the question" to be put to all who fell into the Inquisition's clutches. The priest was forbidden to touch the victim or shed blood. That way his soul remained pure.

BELOW The workings of the Spanish Inquisition. The priest was forbidden to touch those being interrogated but would put "the question" to suspected heretics.

The torture was divided into five stages. Firstly, the suspect was threatened with torture. If that did not have the desired effect, he was dragged and pulled from his cell and shown the instruments of torture—stage two. In the next two stages he was stripped and then strapped onto a rack.

These diabolical machines were common in all torture chambers throughout medieval and Renaissance Europe. Some were horizontal with a windlass at one end. Others were vertical and allowed the victim to be hung by the hands or feet, with weights being attached as the procedure continued. Many of these racks had rotating studded bars placed so that the lower back was contorted backward, adding to the agony.

Once the supposed heretic had been strapped on the rack, the inquisitor asked again for a confession. If this was not forthcoming, he ordered his assistants to begin the final stage, otherwise known as "the question in the first degree."

The suspect was "prolonged," as the process of torture was euphemistically referred to. Pain began in the extremities as he was stretched. Soon limb bones would crack and be pulled out of their sockets. Ligaments and muscles were torn as the pressure slowly intensified. Massive internal damage could be done but as long as no wound was inflicted, no blood would be shed. There were some constraints to the suffering that could be inflicted on the subject; when the victim was to be burned alive, he had to be able to walk to his doom in a public forum. The most skilled torturers could inflict maximum pain but cause little permanent damage.

If the rack did not elicit the confession, a sophisticated form of waterboarding was used. The prisoner was tied to an angled ladder so that the head was lower than the feet. The cranium was held in place by a metal band and all of his limbs and his chest were tightly bound to the ladder. The nostrils were pinched and the mouth was forced open when a metal oval was placed inside. Over this a loose cloth was placed. A flagon of water was then poured into the suspect's mouth. This created a swallowing reaction as both water and cloth were sucked into the poor person's throat, causing them to gasp for breath and nearly asphyxiate. The cloth was then drawn out and the whole process repeated.

ABOVE The rack was used for "the question in the first degree." Suspected heretics were "prolonged" on these fiendish devices.

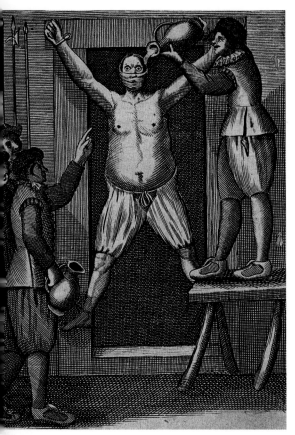

The Inquisition were the first to use waterboarding. It almost never failed to elicit a confession, without inflicting permanent harm on the victim.

RIGHT The auto-da-fé took place on the *quemadero*—the place of burning. Big crowds were attracted to the carnival-like atmosphere of the event.

Centuries earlier, the Church had outlawed repeated torture; a suspected heretic could only be put the question once. But the new Inquisition got around this with a neat legal nicety. The inquisitor, who had to record every procedure and utterance, could choose to "suspend" operations and then resume the procedure again as often and for as long as they desired.

Once a confession had been obtained there were a range of punishments. Some were paraded naked and humiliated; others were fined or exiled. But for those who had converted to Christianity and then relapsed into heresy or for those who had refused to confess, there was one penalty—death. Once the inquisitors had done their job, they handed their prey over to the civil authorities, who were charged with carrying out the required punishments, as the clergy were required to keep their hands clean.

Torquemada's Instructions demanded that these carnivals of death could only be held on the Sabbath or holy holidays. That way a good crowd was sure to turn out. The auto-da-fé began with the accused being lined up in a column outside the dungeons. Those who had confessed and been given the milder punishments such as fines or exile were placed at the head of the column. Behind them came the heretics, who were condemned to death. They were dressed in a cap that was a cross between a modern-day dunce's cap and a bishop's mitre. Around their neck was a rope noose and covering their body was a rough yellow sackcloth. On this were painted scenes of bodies burning in hell while being tormented by devils and demons. If the flames were pointing downward it demonstrated that the prisoner had repented and would be strangled before the flames took hold. If they faced upward it showed they were persistent prisoners who had refused to recant—they would only die when consumed by fire.

The condemned were led to the *quemadero*—the place of burning. Those lapsed Christians who had confessed were tied to their stake and mercifully garroted before the faggots were placed

ABOVE The Spanish Inquisition was untouchable in Spanish society until the advent of Napoleon. This is an auto-da-fé in Plaza Mayor, Madrid, in 1680.

around their feet and set alight. Those who hadn't confessed would die in the flames. Before they were set alight the men were given one more humiliation. A brand was used to light their beards. This was called "shaving the new Christians," and while suffering first-degree burns the heretics got a taste of the burning hell they would soon endure—both on the stake and in Lucifer's domain.

Torquemada's secret society of inquisitors made it their mission to expose the "heretic" *conversos*, with gruesome success. Indeed, toward the end of his tenure, the Grand Inquisitor had overseen the greatest "cleansing" of the lot, when all the Jews of Spain were expelled from the country, using the Alhambra Decree signed by Ferdinand II (1452–1516) and Isabella I (1451–1504) on March 31, 1492. He remained in post until a couple of years before his death on September 16, 1498.

During his reign at least 9,000 heretics had died under his "Instructions." At least 100,000 more had paid fines or been exiled on their path to true Christianity. The Jews had been expelled or converted and for the next several hundred years the secretive Inquisition hunted down heretics until it was closed down for good during the Napoleonic Wars.

THE CATHARS

The Holy Crusades were originally aimed at clearing the Holy Lands of the Middle East of the Moslem Infidels. However, the most bloodthirsty crusade of all was mounted not against Muslims but against fellow Christians. The Albigensian Crusade that raged in southern France from 1209 to 1229 saw large armies attacking Cathar settlements while the Catholic Inquisition used horrific tortures to root out suspected heretics.

The Cathars began as a secret religious society that adopted gnostic (Early Christian) ideas mixed with Eastern mysticism. Even now many of their teachings are shrouded in mystery. The Cathar ideals took off in the Languedoc, an area of France known for its difficult terrain and strong medieval fortresses. From the mid-12th century whole communities began following Cathar ideals. Men and women were considered equal and there may have been aspects of free love involved in some ceremonies. Homosexuality and contraception were not frowned upon. Cathars also tried to abstain from meat and did not condemn the act of suicide. All of these ideals were of course in direct contravention of the teachings of the Catholic Church.

But what earned the secretive sect the title of "the Great Heresy" was their belief that the Catholic Church and its acolytes weren't necessary for personal salvation. The Cathar name for the pope was "the Great Wolf." Even the concept of heaven and hell was doubted, as the Cathars believed in eternal resurrection until personal divinity was attained.

Pope Innocent III saw the Cathars as a real threat and called for a Holy Crusade to expunge them from Christendom. Any knights or nobles who captured Cathar lands were able to keep them and, as in other crusades, death on the battlefield resulted in absolution of sins and a direct path to heaven.

At least one million people were killed in this bloody Christian crusade. Even after large-scale fighting had finished in 1229 the Inquisition led by the Dominican Order maintained a terror state in the region rooting out heretics and burning them at the stake. By 1255 the Cathars and their mysterious practices had been all but wiped out.

RIGHT Many thousands died in the Albigensian Crusade.

THE KNIGHTS TEMPLAR

There are many who believe that the Knights Templar was a unique order of warriors, who during their centuries-long sojourn in Jerusalem were guardians of the most sacred Christian treasures. Their network of castles and brotherhoods across medieval Europe may have safeguarded mythical Christian relics such as the Ark of the Covenant, the Holy Grail, and the Blood of Jesus Christ. Many potboilers have been written that seem to make these ideas fact. But there is another, darker view of the order, which paints them as a coven of homosexual devil worshippers who used their power and influence to engage in horrific heresies and possibly even human sacrifice.

The truth may be somewhere in the middle. Even today Catholic brotherhoods are rocked worldwide by accusations—some proven—of pedophilia, rape, and other sexual crimes.

The Knights Templar (otherwise known as the Poor Knights of the Temple of Solomon) were founded by Hugues de Payens (1070–1136) and eight other knights in 1118 or 1119, resolving to live in poverty and chastity. He was a veteran of the First Crusade (1096–99) and had seen that many pilgrims to Jerusalem were being robbed and attacked. King Baldwin II (1060–1131) officially endorsed the order by giving them the Al-Aqsa Mosque near the Dome of the Rock on the Temple Mount. This was the original site of the Temple of Solomon and one of the holiest sites in the Middle East to Christians, Muslims, and Jews. Much of the mythology surrounding the Knights Templar hints at what they may have excavated while at this most holy location.

BELOW Al-Aqsa Mosque on Temple Mount, Jerusalem. It is at this site that the Knights Templar are reputed to have found the Holy Grail.

The order was formally recognized by the Pope in January 1128, in awarding them their own distinctive dress of a plain white robe, to which in 1147 a red cross was added. The Templar Rule was also handed down. This gave the master total power over the order until his death. The knights were supposed to embody pure chivalry and self-sacrifice. They were not allowed to consort in any way with women and had to remain celibate. They were forbidden to kiss mothers, wives, sisters, or indeed any women at all, and if the Knight was married before joining the order, his wife had to join a nunnery. They spent their days like Benedictine monks: praying, eating in silence, saying paternosters, and dressing without personal adornment. They also did extensive weapons training, becoming proficient with dirk, sword, mace, crossbow, and axe.

Not that everyone who wanted to join the order made it that far. The chapter delved deeply into the background of any applicant, and his character was rigorously tested. Then, if he cleared those hurdles, in a highly secret swearing-in ceremony the entrant was required to swear an oath of obedience to the master and the rule, promising to live a life of poverty and chastity. Most importantly, the vows included a promise to protect Jerusalem from the heathens. It was the secrecy of this swearing-in ceremony that led to many foul rumors circulating as to what the order got up to—rumors that Philip IV (1268–1314) would exploit to the full.

ABOVE **Philip IV. The cash-strapped monarch used rumors of homosexual free-for-alls to arrest the Knights Templar and seize their immeasurable wealth.**

The rules were rigorously enforced. Anyone who broke them could be forced to eat from the floor for a year or even executed by being walled up in one of the many Templar forts. As a result of such privations, the Knights were initially seen as perfect paragons of Christian purity. However, their role as protector of pilgrims ultimately led to their downfall as their image became tarnished with a most unknightly activity—banking. Pilgrimage to the Holy Lands was a dangerous business and pilgrims put their life, and their savings, on the line. Pilgrims and knights journeying to the Holy Land would deposit their monies in a Templar castle in their home town in exchange for a bill of credit—the earliest form of cheque. They would then redeem the cash once in Palestine.

This simple transfer business soon grew until the Templars had a huge financial concern on their hands. They were given wills and acted as executors. Huge amounts of money and wealth were deposited in castles, and many sought to save their souls by bequeathing fortunes to the order. Eventually the order became crucial to the French monarchy and other rulers. They collected taxes, paid pensions, and even safeguarded the British Crown Jewels. A network of castles spread across Europe as gradually they acquired tremendous wealth.

Rumors also abounded regarding what the Templars extracted from the Holy land. The Holy Grail and many other relics were suspected to have been smuggled out of Jerusalem and taken to Templar headquarters in France and England. The rumor mill also suggested that not entirely Christian practices were being followed in the mysterious lodges where the Templars lived.

By the early 14th century the Knights Templar had grown from a tiny organization of nine impoverished knights to a network of financial power reaching every corner of Europe. They even diversified into massive farming estates generating even more wealth. Personnel numbered in the tens of thousands, though only a small proportion of these were fighting brothers. Most were lay knights or attendants concerned with cooking, cleaning, and, of course, counting.

BELOW The Grand Master Jacques de Molay was not spared. Hot pincers were used to tear strips of skin off his inner thighs and buttocks.

There was one big fly in the spiritual ointment. The very reason for the knights' existence had passed. The Christians had been booted out of the Holy Land and the Crusades were over. In 1291, Muslims conquered the last Crusader state, based on Acre. Soon after, the last Templars left.

Today, Friday the 13th is universally seen as a day when bad things can happen. This was not always the case. But when the Templar order was all but eliminated on Friday October 13, 1307, the date became a resounding ill omen.

The Templars had become a rule unto themselves. Despite the fall of their possessions in the Holy Lands of Outremer (the Middle East), they still had at least 870 castles and preceptories. Papal dispensations meant they were exempted from paying royal taxes, and such was the size and strength of their army they were seen as a threatening independent military power in the midst of Europe. Many resented them.

ABOVE **Krak des Chevaliers in Syria. Even the mightiest castles fell to the Muslims. Once removed from the Holy Lands the Knights Templar were not needed.**

Philip IV was crowned King of France in 1285. He inherited a kingdom in great financial difficulty. For many years the King sought to stabilize the French economy and expand his powerbase. In 1306, he sought to raise extra revenue, and taxes tripled as a result. Riots broke out, and such was the fury of Parisians, Philip had to take refuge in the Paris Temple. For three days the Knights Templar protected him from the mob—a kindness they would soon have cause to regret.

During this time Philip was no doubt reminded of the great wealth of the Templars; it is likely that he saw the solution to his financial problems during these three days. Guillaume de Nogaret (1260–1313), Philip's enforcer, came up with a scheme to solve his financial problems once and for all. They would arrest the Templars, convict them of heresy and seize the order's assets.

Philip's moves against the Templars rivaled in efficiency Hitler's Night of the Long Knives. On September 14, 1307, hundreds of couriers issued from Paris. The sealed instructions they carried to his closest allies and enforcers throughout France set out plans for the crackdown to come. At dawn on October 13, 1307, warrants of arrest were issued for every Templar in France. The warrants accused the holy order of the vilest heresies and within the space of a few hours almost 5,000 Templars the length and breadth of the country had been taken into custody. Only 20 or so managed to escape the roundup. Such a dire portrait of the Templars was painted that no sheriff could dare resist arresting their prey.

Philip followed up this 'shock and awe' assault upon the Templars with a publicity campaign that rivals modern-day politics. On September 15th, in every town and village in France, Dominican friars and royal representatives regaled the population

ABOVE Many Templars confessed and were let off with minor punishments. Others felt the full vengeance of the French church and were burned to death.

with sordid stories of buggery and depravity. On the 16th, Philip sent letters to his fellow kings and princes throughout Europe, explaining his actions and urging them to follow his lead.

Philip had set the scene; now he had to back up his actions. To help him he had a legion of inquisitors itching to tear the worst confessions from Templar throats. Along with the usual methods used by inquisitors the French had developed a particularly nasty torture. Pig fat was smeared on the soles of the suspect's feet, and he was then suspended above some flames. This slow-cooked the feet like a pig on the spit; one Templar Priest was shocked when his bones fell out of his feet several days after the torture had concluded. And unlike the Spanish Inquisition the French had no prohibition against the shedding of blood. The Grand Master de Molay (1244–1314) wrote of how skin was torn from his inner thighs, belly, and back.

The crimes the order confessed to were horrible. The induction ceremony supposedly required new recruits to spit on the cross and deny Christ. A four-faced head complete with devil's horns was worshipped as a pagan idol, and many confessed to kissing the "receptor" mouth, navel, stomach, buttocks, or penis. Once inducted as a full member of the order, it was apparently improper to refuse a brother's sexual advances, according to what was confessed. In fact, the confessions were remarkably similar, and it is obvious the French inquisitors put words in the mouths of the brethren as they were tortured. Many retracted the confessions, even though retraction meant being burned at the stake.

The damage had been done. The Pope supported Philip's campaign and Templars throughout Europe were arrested and tortured. Templar lands and assets were seized, and huge amounts of wealth were soon flowing into the French royal coffers. But Philip did not have it all his own way. Indeed, perhaps the Templars did possess some relic that gave them supernatural powers.

On March 18, 1314 de Molay was consigned to the flames. He cursed Guillaume de Nogaret to die within eight days, the Pope was given forty days, and within a year, screamed Molay, Philip himself would die. One week later de Nogaret died. Pope Clement V lived for 33 more days. Philip died eight months later.

Some lodges survived the purges, and if for a minute we suspend our modern skepticism, it is possible to imagine that in a secret den in the heart of Scotland the Knights Templar still stand guard over Christ's Blood, the Holy Grail, and the Ark of the Covenant.

The Templars in Battle

The superior training and discipline of the holy orders of knights made them indispensable to victories in Outremer. While other knights lacked discipline and would charge the Saracen armies without orders, the Knights Templar were bound to obey the commands of their grand master. This made the Knights Templar battle winners.

The Battle of Montgisard on November 25, 1177, was fought between the Ayyubids under Saladin (1137–93) and forces from the Kingdom of Jerusalem under King Baldwin IV (1161–85). The Christian forces deployed 374 knights and 80 Templars supported by several thousand infantry armed with crossbows and spears. They were faced by perhaps 26,000 Saracens.

The two armies deployed with the smaller Christian army overlapped on both flanks. However, the Muslim cavalry was tired out from plundering the surrounding area and Baldwin decided to go straight through their center.

First he sent the Bishop of Bethlehem to ride forward with a relic of the True Cross. Baldwin then prostrated himself before the sacred item and prayed for victory. He then arranged the mounted troops in battle order. At their center was Odo of St. Amand (1110–79) and his 80 Templars. These formed a mailed fist in the center of the line (some suggest in wedge formation). The knights galloped forward and split the center of Saladin's line, causing the Muslim forces to flee in disarray. None could resist the armored might of the Templars. Saladin managed to escape on a camel and the Crusaders captured his entire baggage train.

RIGHT **At the Battle of Montgisard the superior discipline, armor, and weaponry of the Templars helped put the Saracens to flight.**

THE ILLUMINATI

There are more conspiracy theories regarding the Illuminati than almost any other secret organization. They originally began as a splinter group within the Freemasons but then came to dominate every aspect of the many lodges in which they had a presence. They are a prime focus for conspiracy theorists and have been blamed for economic disasters, revolutions, and wars. In fact, it seems that though the Illuminati don't currently exist, the fascination with them remains, with many of their symbols still being seen today. What is more, when they were a powerful force, it seems that they were also wholly preoccupied with improving society. The Illuminati can be called the children of the Enlightenment.

The Age of Enlightenment (also known as the Age of Reason) was a European movement that took hold in the 18th century. The bloody religious battles of the 16th and 17th centuries, coupled with scientific advances, led many European intellectuals to question the structure of society, which rested upon the divine right of kings, church, and nobles to hold the rest of the population in abject servitude.

Reason and logic were seen as superior to superstitions, and ideals such as liberty, tolerance, fraternity, equality, and democracy were explored. At the heart of Enlightenment thinking was a desire to improve the lot of humankind.

Francis Bacon (1561–1626), René Descartes (1596–1650), John Locke (1632–1704), Voltaire (1694–1778), and Jean-Jacques Rousseau (1712–1778) were some of the leading lights of enlightenment thought.

In his famous book, *The Social Contract* (1762), Rousseau wrote, "Man is born free and everywhere he is in chains." Of course, Rousseau was writing both literally and symbolically. Man was chained to his class in society and was locked into an ignorant state through lack of education. It was this ignorance borne of superstition and tradition on which the Illuminati sought to shine a light.

BELOW Jean Jacques Rousseau was an influential thinker of the Age of Enlightenment. He considered the divine right of kings to be a superstition.

Adam Weishaupt (1748–1830) was the founder of the Bavarian Illuminati. Born in the lovely town of Ingolstadt in the south of the German state of Bavaria, he soon proved to be a brilliant intellect. Raised upon Enlightenment writing, by the age of 27 he had been promoted to the post of Dean of Canon Law at Ingolstadt University.

Like many of his generation he was enrolled in the Rite of Strict Observance followed by Freemasonry. This section of Freemasons believes in strict observance of Masonic rituals before an individual can progress within the organization. Not possessing the friendly bonhomie of other lodges, the Strict Observance lodges stick to the letter of the law. However, as with all lodges, religion and politics could not be discussed. This made the Freemasons largely passive observers of society.

ABOVE Adam Weishaupt, founder of the Bavarian Illuminati. He used the Masonic lodges to spread a radical creed that sought to dispense with Christianity and nationalism.

Weishaupt wanted to use the knowledge and rituals of Freemasonry to take an active role in freeing society from the domination of the church and a social hierarchy based on bloodlines. He wanted to emancipate humanity. To achieve this, on May 1, 1776, he founded the Order of the Illuminati.

The brilliance of Weishaupt's idea was not to make the Illuminati a rival organization to the Freemasons but to actually use his powerful allies to take over lodges throughout Europe. He recruited grand masters into his new organization, who would then recruit from their own lodges. Soon lodges throughout Europe were dominated by the Illuminati, though not all masons could join. Those who held firm beliefs would be offended by the anti-Christian stance of the new secret society.

The aims of the organization were manifold. They wanted to rid European society of Christianity and nationalism. These were to be replaced with a pan-European republic. Human rights would be enshrined in law and each individual would be able to rise within society based on his own merit—meritocracy as an explicit form of social progress rather than the stifling aristocracy that prevailed at the time. Jesus was portrayed as the original grand master of the Illuminati, as he sought to free humanity from the yoke of empire.

ABOVE The Eye of Providence, the enduring symbol of the Illuminati. It could only be worn by senior members of this progressive secret society.

To maintain secrecy, the Illuminati gave themselves pseudonyms from antiquity and never referred to each other by title. Countries and cities were renamed, with many terms encrypted, including days and months. Years were altered, with 630 CE now seen as year 1 (the year chosen, seemingly randomly, to confuse all who tried to read secret documents). Secret signs and handshakes such as those employed by the Masons, but subtly different, were used for recognition.

In pursuance of their aims the Illuminati began ridiculing the church and nobility throughout Europe. Many funds were diverted into Illuminati coffers, and this money was used for publishing leaflets and pamphlets attacking the church. University professors, government administrators, and even members of the clergy were actively involved in spreading Illuminati propaganda. Articles ridiculing leading public figures and exposing their crimes were widely distributed.

The organization had a strongly spiritual side. By undergoing a complex series of rituals and insights an individual could clear out the clutter from their mind, repudiate preconceptions, prejudices, and fears, and move into an exalted, transcendental spiritual state. Unique among the many societies of the time, women, too, were welcomed into

BY UNDERGOING A COMPLEX SERIES OF RITUALS AND INSIGHTS
AN INDIVIDUAL COULD CLEAR OUT THE CLUTTER FROM THEIR MIND,
REPUDIATE PRECONCEPTIONS, PREJUDICES, AND FEARS, AND MOVE
INTO AN EXALTED, TRANSCENDENTAL SPIRITUAL STATE.

its ranks. It was while moving through these stages toward spiritual enlightenment that the Illuminati taught symbolism, and these symbols are still in use today.

The thinking utilized by the Illuminati is remarkably like psychotherapy today. As the adherent moved through a process of self-inquiry, they were to examine their past for traumas and formative experiences that placed preconceptions and limitations in their mind. By clearing out these negative blockages they could move toward a stage of "gnosis" or spiritual oneness with the heavens.

The Illuminati motto was, "Let there be light, and there shall be light." So through self-awareness an individual could become one with the divine forces of the universe just as by examining society and realizing social problems rooted in the past, these could also be eliminated, leading to a utopian society.

The Illuminati were not a dark secret society with an agenda of fear and terror, but rather the opposite. To attain enlightenment, a series of proscribed steps had to be followed and completed:

BELOW **Wolfgang Amadeus Mozart was a member of the Illuminati. Had his membership been revealed when he was alive, it is possible he would have lost many of his patrons.**

first the four steps of the Nursery Degrees: Preparation, Novice, Minerval, and Lesser Illuminatus. After this came the three stages of the Symbolic Masonry Degree followed by the three stages of the Scotch Masonry Degree. These were followed by the two stages of the Lesser Mysteries Degrees and finally the Greater Mysteries Degrees, culminating in the two highest degrees, Magus and Rex.

The Minerval degree was perhaps the most important, as this was when members were asked to sign an oath of obligation to the order, committing them to purifying the intellect. Once they had passed this level, the inductee could wear the all-seeing eye or Eye of Providence—the eye on top of a pyramid beloved of so many conspiracy theories.

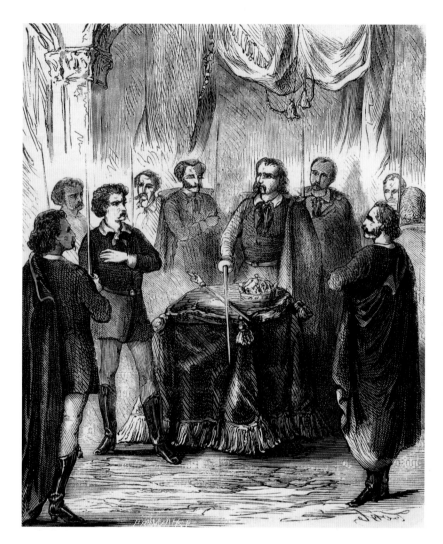

ABOVE **Even now the complicated rituals of the Illuminati remain shrouded in mystery. Much learning was required to ascend through the different levels.**

Within the space of a few decades the Illuminati could boast some 2,500 members, including luminaries such as Wolfgang Amadeus Mozart (1756–91). However, the success led to complaints and resentment, with several university professors in Munich being arrested. Admitting they were members of the order, they confessed that they did not follow Christianity but they did believe that suicide was not a sin.

Masons realized that their lodges had in many instances been hijacked by the agnostic organization and sought to expel the rival members. In Bavaria all secret societies were banned in a series of laws beginning in 1785, and the movement was disbanded. Or was it?

The Rosicrucians

Not a lot is known about this shadowy organization. It was founded in the early 15th century by Christian Rosenkreuz (1378–1484), who sought to blend spirituality and the occult with alchemy. The goal was to bring about a global transformation. He set up a secret society separate from the Christian Church and thus became the model for many subsequent societies such as the Freemasons and the Illuminati.

The basis of Rosicrucian thought can be found in two manifestos published in Germany in the early 17th century. *The Fame of the Brotherhood of Rosicrucian* and *The Confession of the Brotherhood of the*

Rosicrucian are typically obtuse and mysterious, so that any devotee can extract whatever message they would like to hear.

The publication of the Manifestos two centuries later has led many to believe that the Rosicrucians have been behind every scientific and political revolution of modern times.

RIGHT **The rites of Rosicrucian ceremonies are still shrouded in mystery. Nevertheless, it is likely that they appealed to a well-to-do membership.**

Many Illuminati remained in positions of power, with Weishaupt becoming a professor of philosophy at the University of Göttingen. He seemed to lead a low-key life, but some theories say the movement continued its work as an underground organization. Indeed, many leading lights of the French Revolution were supposed to hail from this sacred order. At first they sought to put Illuminati ideals into place, but the violent excesses of the Terror soon discredited the movement and perhaps signaled its death knell.

If the movement did go underground and its members are still engaged in trying to create a worldwide spiritual and physical utopia, they are not doing a very good job.

FREEMASONS

Nowadays the Freemasons are seen as a fairly harmless organization more committed to doing good deeds than dominating society. But their press hasn't always been so positive.

Many individuals have survived sticky situations solely because of their membership of this mysterious group. One French officer was captured by Russian Cossacks during the Great Retreat from Moscow in 1812. Along with hundreds of comrades, he was stripped of the last dregs of his clothing and placed in a barn, where they watched as the Cossacks sold them to Russian peasants for a kopek each. They well knew their fate if the peasants ever got their hands on them. Many a captured Frenchman had been buried alive in a freezing privy or had their head bashed in while tied to a fallen log.

The captain saw a group of Russian Guards infantry officers pass by and in a last desperate attempt at survival got their attention by making a Masonic gesture. An hour later he was clothed and fed and speeding his way to a comfortable imprisonment in a covered droshky. One of the Russian officers had recognized the sign and hauled the relieved Frenchman aside. None of the other invaders were as fortunate, and no doubt many met unpleasant ends at the hands of the outraged peasants.

BELOW Many signatories to the Declaration of Independence were members of the Freemasons. George Washington is depicted here in his Freemason apron.

In World War Two Freemasons weren't so lucky. As many as 200,000 Masons were put in the gas chambers by Hitler because he feared they were a secret powerbase. After the Germans invaded the Channel Islands, the Freemasons' Hall was ransacked and lodge members deported to the camps.

There are many stories about the growth of the Freemasons. They use symbols from Ancient Babylon, Egypt, and Rome and would no doubt like to imagine a lineage stretching that far back into the past. However, it is more likely that the Freemasons evolved from the community of Masons, a wandering elite during the Middle Ages. Tasked with building the immense cathedrals and castles of the period, it was essential that they accumulated a great store of skill and knowledge, but also

that they guarded knowledge of their specialist skills. Complex signs and tokens were developed to ensure that Masons developed the craft and could recognize others with the same abilities.

The first historical record of the Masons as we know them today appears in 1717 when the first Grand Lodge of London was founded. From here lodges spread throughout Europe, creating an international brotherhood with strict hierarchies and secrets. With such a diverse number of lodges it was possible for many to indulge in arcane and downright evil practices, such as procuring youths for pedophile rings. However, now they are largely a harmless group of lodges whose key aim is charitable work—plus the occasional bit of goat-riding, of course.

ABOVE **The Freemasons' Hall in London. Many edifices such as this one still exist to testify to the dominance that this mutual society once held.**

Masonic Terms in Common Use

Nowadays there are still many lodges around the world and they continue to play an active role in society. Many common terms in use today come from freemasonry. For instance:

"On the level" means all equal in the brotherhood, regardless of background. It is also related to the basic masonry skill of producing accurate right angles and smooth stone, which requires skill and training to achieve.

"Hoodwinked" now means to have been deceived but comes from hooded wink-closed eyes—a part of the ceremony performed when someone, covered in black cloth, moves from one level to another.

"Blackballed" now refers to somebody being refused entry to a club or permanently shamed. It comes from the initiation procedure for new members. If a new recruit was proposed by an existing brother, the lodge would be informed of the individual's background and history. His induction would be voted on by placing marbles within a box. If any knew of a dark secret or poor behavior in the initiate's past, he put a black ball in the box rather than a white ball. If only one in hundreds was black, that was enough. Entry was refused as the candidate had been "blackballed."

"Token of affection" relates to known handshakes.

BELOW **A range of Freemason objects and paraphernalia. Different badges, awards, and symbols place members within the order's hierarchy.**

THE ELDERS OF ZION

As far as secret societies and world conspiracies go, this was a humdinger. An imaginary humdinger. A Russian mystic called Sergei Nilus (1862–1929) wrote in 1903 how he came upon the minutes of the First Zionist Congress, held in Basel, Switzerland, in 1907. Sergei rather grandiloquently titled these minutes *The Protocols of the Elders of Zion*.

Including such dramatic statements as "The Gentiles are our sheep, we are the wolves," the Protocols were meant to be the work of 300 elders whose identities were kept secret even from their Jewish brethren. The elders discussed in great detail how through agencies such as the Masonic League they kept the world in thrall to their dark designs. They gleefully described how they had weakened the goyim (non-Jews) through crime networks, alcohol, drug use, and false religions, leading to weakened and inferior races.

By controlling the media, education networks (especially academics in universities), and corrupt politicians they would lead to the goyim adopting dangerous liberal ideals. Money and trade were to be elevated above Christianity, and the Gentiles would turn from religion to greed. The states would then take on ruinous amounts of debt and bankrupt themselves, allowing the Jewish leaders to take over the reins of world power.

ABOVE **Henry Ford was an enthusiastic proponent of the anti-Semitic tract *The Protocols of the Elders of Zion*.**

The industrialist Henry Ford (1863–1947) swallowed this tosh hook, line, and sinker, and in 1920 serialized the Russian document in a newspaper he owned. The articles were combined in a book titled *The International Jew: The World's Foremost Problem*. Many anti-Semites—including Adolf Hitler—read these texts and worked them into their worldview. The Nazi tabloid *Der Stürmer*, written by Hitler's chief Jew-baiter, Julius Striecher (1885–1946), often drew on the Protocols for its anti-Semitic rants.

In 1921, they were exposed as a fake by *The Times* newspaper, and it has long been assumed that members of the Tsar's secret police, the Okhrana, cobbled them together from a variety of sources. The Okhrana had a long history of seeking to blame Russians' woes on the Jewish minority, so as to protect the Romanovs.

Nevertheless, Ford stuck to his guns and never gave up his belief in the vast Jewish conspiracy.

THE HELLFIRE CLUBS

There are many Hellfire clubs still in existence. One that was open in Melbourne for about 20 years was known as a bastion of hard drinking and sadomasochistic sex. The first Hellfire clubs were pretty much the same.

The original Hellfire Club was founded in 1719 by Philip, Duke of Wharton (1698–1731). Two years later a royal decree was handed down banning it, which pretty much summed up what the club was about: blasphemy, insulting sacred objects, abusing God, and corrupting the minds and morals of young women.

The best-known Hellfire Club was the one that Sir Francis Dashwood (1708–81) and the 4th Earl of Sandwich (1718–92) frequented in the 1730s. It initially met in the George and Vulture Inn in London but soon moved into a complex of subterranean spaces now known as the Hellfire Caves. Many influential figures were inducted into the club including Benjamin Franklin (1706–1790), William Hogarth (1697–1764), and Frederick, Prince of Wales (1707–51). It seems it was basically a drinking club, but when it moved underground into the caves the motto 'Fais ce que tu voudras' (Do what thou wilt) took on a new meaning. The caves were decorated with pagan symbols complete with giant phalluses and sacrificial altars. Bacchus and Venus were worshipped in rollicking ceremonies that involved food, alcohol, candles, robes, and masks. Of course, a lot of the local lasses were put in the mix but the only thing that was sacrificed was their virginity. Meetings were held twice a month and ritual clothing was worn. Later on, accusations of Satanism were levelled at the club, but this is unlikely, being way too serious for what amounted to upper-class debauchery in an atmospheric setting.

LEFT Philip the 1st Duke of Wharton enjoyed blasphemy, getting drunk, and corrupting the minds and morals of young women in his spare time.

THE INDEPENDENT ORDER OF ODD FELLOWS

This order's symbol of the three rings encapsulates the international motto of this benign group, "*Amicitia, Amor et Veritas*," which translates as "Friendship, Love, and Truth." One or two words should perhaps be added to this motto, such as conviviality and consumption. It seems that the original order was more of a drinking club than anything else, and this benign beginning has informed the organization ever since. Through the many years of their existence the Odd Fellows saw themselves as almost a caricature of more serious organizations such as the Freemasons.

During the later Middle Ages and the Renaissance era, guilds and banking houses became powerful forces within society. The rise of the Masons and their conversion into the powerful secret society of Freemasonry is indicative of this concentration of power into organized bodies. Guilds were run by "masters," who restricted membership and

BELOW **A 1917 badge signifying membership of the Independent Order of Odd Fellows. The three rings symbolize "Friendship, Love, and Truth."**

ABOVE **This illustration shows a member of Odd Fellows in his full garb. The similarity to Mason insignia is clear.**

concentrated privileges in their own hands. As a response to the domination of the "masters," the "fellows," who were lower on the rung of training and accreditation, set up their own loose organizations, in which they could gather and help out their associates. Guilds would only allow members from one profession to join, but any "odd fellow" from any trade was allowed to join the new organization.

The Odd Fellows refuse to take themselves too seriously, and many esoteric tales have been told to explain their origins. Just as the Masons tie their past to Ancient Sumer, the Odd Fellows have explained that they are in fact descended from Roman legionaries. According to this rather imaginative origin story, a group of soldiers under Nero (37–68 CE) formed the first association in 55 CE. They were then given official recognition as "Odd-Fellow" by Emperor Titus in 79 CE. From there they spread into Spain, Portugal, and then, by the 12th century, England and France. Another creation myth sees them as an ancient Germanic order which continued from pagan times with pagan rites that inspired the resistance against the Romans in the Battle of the Teutoburg Forest in 9 CE.

While these creation myths are probably alcohol-related, there may be a kernel of truth within them. The first surviving documentary evidence of the Odd Fellows is the minutes of a meeting held during 1748 by Lodge 9 of the Loyal Aristarchus Odd Fellow Lodge, held at the Globe Tavern, although an earlier mention of the organization has them meeting in the Oakley Arms in Southwark, London, in 1745. Most of the references to lodges throughout England have them meeting in pubs and hotels. They often mention members of the constabulary being called out to put down drunken disturbances.

In the latter part of the 18th century, two orders of Odd Fellows competed for members. The Order of Patriotic Odd Fellows and The Ancient Order of Odd Fellows eventually buried their differences and merged into the Grand United Order of Odd Fellows. They soon spread across the Atlantic, where the first American chapter opened in Baltimore, Maryland, in 1819 under the title of the Independent Order of Odd Fellows. True to their early chapters' tolerant beginnings, the Odd Fellows have always been progressive. The first chapter for African Americans was founded in New York City in the 1830s, while the Odd Fellows Daughters of America branches were set up for female membership in the 1850s.

Like the Freemasons the order has many secret handshakes and symbols to denote membership. It also has a ritual for initiation which still remains shrouded in mystery. An eyewitness account might read as follows:

The lodge's reception hall was decked with candles and drapes. All of the brothers were present and each wore a mask to hide their identity. The Master wore a white band around his face with a wig placed on top. He also wore a white apron made of kid leather with scarlet trim. Few other signs of hierarchy were evident for what is largely a convivial brotherhood. The initiate was ushered into this solemn space and there blindfolded. After a long pause where he could only hear the flickering of the candles and the hushed breath of the brothers the candidate was ordered to stand. Around him rose a hubbub of clashing chains and other mysterious sounds produced to confound the initiate and test his mettle. The sounds became physical as a bucket of chilled water was poured upon his masked head and he was gently thrashed with brushwood. The climax of the ceremony came when the mask was whipped from the initiate's head to allow him to see a sword held up with its tip poised to tear into his chest. In this position he was charged with upholding the lodge's principles to the day of his death.

No doubt this harmless fun was recounted in many a late-night drinking session, and any fear or anxiety displayed by the new member would be the topic of humorous anecdotes for years afterward. The Odd Fellows are not so obsessed with advancement and levels as their cousins in the Freemasons, and it is largely a convivial club concerned with good works and mutual insurance. Pensions are paid to the widows of dead members, and funds are set aside for funeral expenses or for payment to members who might temporarily be down on their luck and facing unemployment. Of course, the mutual assistance given to each member in finding job and business opportunities remains paramount.

MOST OF THE REFERENCES TO LODGES THROUGHOUT ENGLAND HAVE THEM MEETING IN PUBS AND HOTELS. THEY OFTEN MENTION MEMBERS OF THE CONSTABULARY BEING CALLED OUT TO PUT DOWN DRUNKEN DISTURBANCES.

BELOW British-born American philanthropist Thomas Wildey (1782–1861), founder of the Independent Order of Odd Fellows, the American incarnation of the British Odd Fellows.

Nevertheless, not all would be admitted. When a new member sought to join they had to prove that they and their family were of sound health, both physically and financially, and possessed of the correct moral character. Applicants were then voted on by other members and a method of white-ball or black-ball ballot similar to that of the Freemasons was used. But as in all things with this order they a showed greater degree of tolerance, and three black balls, rather than one, were required to block membership. Those who voted against membership were often asked to explain the reasoning behind their decision. Once this had been obtained another vote was held and this second result was final.

The modern-day lodges term themselves IOOF (The Independent Order of Odd Fellows) and maintain a presence in Australia, Mexico, the Philippines, Cuba, Venezuela, Chile, Norway, Denmark, and Finland, among many others. They are chiefly concerned with good works, self-awareness, and networking across national barriers. However, numbers continue to drop and, like Masonic halls around the world, many of their lodges are passing into private hands.

RIGHT King George IV of the United Kingdom (1762–1830) enjoyed membership of both the Odd Fellows and the Freemasons.

THE HOLY VEHM

Vigilante groups are common where ordinary people feel threatened by lawlessness and rampant crime. The ultimate prototype for a secret vigilante organization would have to be the Vehm, which began as a crime-fighting society in medieval Germany under the strictest of vows: new members had to pledge that they and their families would commit suicide if they ever revealed the secrets of their order. The function of the Vehm was to bring to secret trial, and pass sentence on, wrongdoers—the sentence almost invariably being death.

Even today members of the Holy Vehm may still be found in Germany. If you happen to see somebody at a restaurant aligning all of their cutlery so it is pointed to the center of the table like the spokes of a wheel, it is a member of this ancient order displaying his membership to other initiates.

During the Middle Ages Germany was divided into hundreds of principalities, which allowed bandits and criminals to flee into neighboring jurisdictions to avoid punishment for even the most heinous crimes. This led to many areas of Germany being plunged into lawlessness, and in the 13th century no region was worse than Westphalia, between the rivers Rhine and Weser. Unemployed mercenaries, robber barons, and bands of outlaws roamed the wooded countryside robbing, stealing, and extorting from the local peasants. Freemen and guildsmen could take it no longer and so formed the Chivalrous Order of the Holy Vehm. Vehm can be loosely translated as "agreed law," and with church backing they armed themselves and in mounted packs hunted down, passed judgment on, and inevitably killed any thieves or murderers they encountered. The Vehm had a strict hierarchy. At the top were the *Stuhlherren* (the judges). Next were the *Freischöffen* (deputy judges) and below them the *Frohnboten* (the executioners). They sought to protect themselves with elaborate rituals to guarantee secrecy. Any new member was initiated into a local "court" in the dead of night and had to swear to kill himself and his family if he should reveal himself to be a member of the order.

To seal the pact, the *Stuhlherr* (judge) would draw a blade across the initiate's throat, drawing a trickle of blood as a warning of what could come should the order be betrayed. The new member then kissed the cross of the sword and swore fealty to the tribunal and its judgments. He swore that nothing would prevent him from carrying out any sentences passed, and he would respect none except for the emperor if they sought to impede an execution. The new member, who could not even tell his family of the new association, was then given a length of rope and a dagger with the letters S.S.G.G., the initial letters of the Vehm's motto, *Stock, Stein, Gras, Grein* (sticks, stones, grass, tears). The penalty for breaking

RIGHT **The Court of the Holy Vehm. Once it pronounced a sentence of death there was no escape. Specialist killers would pursue their prey for years.**

ABOVE The Vehm pronounce judgement on an accused man. The executioner stands at the rear with his beheading sword, ready to carry out the sentence.

faith was extreme. The offender would have his eyes torn from his sockets, and his tongue would be cut out and thrown into the flames before he was hung from the tallest tree as a warning to others.

Once sworn in, the member could participate in the "forbidden courts" and carry out summary justice on any who fell foul of the Holy Vehm. The courts met in the dead of night in sacred groves, in caves, or by river banks. S.S.G.G. would be chiseled into the side of a rock or a tree trunk to show the location of the tribunal and its sacred role. Criminals and lawbreakers were summoned to the courts. If they did not attend, they were found guilty. Others had sentence passed without even a summons, and the first they knew of their fate was being hauled from their horse by a gang of armed men or pulled from their bed as they slept.

The sentence was always carried out in the same brutal way. A rope was strung over a high limb and the condemned prisoner kicked and gasped his life out as he was hauled up at the end of a noose. At dawn passers-by might come across the swinging cadaver. Invariably planted in the ground below the swinging corpse would be a dagger with S.S.G.G. carved into the hilt. "*Vehmgericht*," the peasants would mutter. The Vehm court. None dared touch the corpse. Any individual who sought to protect an accused man, or testify on his behalf, or even seek to bury the dead body, could earn themselves the same fate.

None could escape the judgment of the fell court. The judge would take his symbolic rope and throw it beyond the Vehm circle. He then condemned the victim with this oath: "I now curse his foul blood, flesh, and soul. His body may never be buried but it must be blown away by the wind. Or else birds of prey, crows, and ravens can consume and destroy him. Beasts of the land can consume him. I send his soul to the dear Lord for him to receive if he chooses to do so."

It was forbidden for any of the Vehm to tell of a sentence, though no doubt gossip leaked out. Many tried to flee judgment but to no avail. Specially tasked *Frohnboten* would be given a target and as much time and as many funds as were required to carry out the deed. Even knights or nobles in their castles had reason to fear, for eventually, when their guard dropped, a *Frohnboten* would be there to carry out the sentence, even decades later.

BELOW Emperor Maximilian I saw the Holy Vehm as a challenge to his powers and sought to stamp them out.

Within the space of a few decades, hundreds of thousands had joined the ranks of the Vehm and the original goal of ridding Westphalia of freebooting bandits had been achieved. Courts began to exceed their original remit and soon thousands of innocents were dying on trumped-up charges of heresy or theft. Churchmen and citizens began to complain, and under Emperor Maximilian I (1459–1519) rules were passed outlawing their acts. The strengthening of the rule of law in most German principalities and duchies rendered the Vehm courts largely irrelevant, and by the end of the 16th century they had been forced underground.

Then in 1811 membership was banned under the ruler Jerome-Napoleon Bonaparte (1784–1860). However, it seems that the Vehm continued all the same, and had a brief resurgence as an anti-Jewish organization during the Nazi era. There may even be some active cells today, though what they get up to is perhaps best not to contemplate.

THE PRIORY OF SION

The Priory of Sion was established in Jerusalem in 1099. It had one goal, to protect and find documentation that proved the Merovingian royal line were the descendants of Jesus Christ and Mary Magdalene, his legal wife. Mary Magdalene was the original Holy Grail, or at least her womb was, the origin of the precious bloodlines of Jesus's descendants. The Priory of Sion founded the Knights Templar as its military and financial arm to carry out the task of placing members of the Merovingian royal dynasty on every throne in Europe.

BELOW **Jesus and Mary as depicted by Titian. The inventors of the Priory of Sion made up a wondrous tale about the pair's offspring.**

While based in Jerusalem, the Priory of Sion found documents proving that Jesus Christ was human, not divine, despite being descended from the Hebrew Davidic royal line. According to the story, he and Mary had produced several heirs. Rather than dying on the Cross Jesus had carted Mary and their children off to France, where their bloodlines had established the Merovingian royal dynasty which had ruled the Franks from 457 to 751.

The documents found by the Priory were earth-shattering. Many original texts by Jesus and his followers portrayed him as a wholly human teacher. Most explosive of all were the writings of Mary, detailing her relationship with Jesus and her journey to France. These officially debunked the Catholic story that Christ was divine and the Popes were his spiritual representatives on earth.

Unsurprisingly, the powers-that-be in the Vatican were not happy with this revisionism, which rendered meaningless their *raison d'être* and put the massive spiritual empire of the Catholic Church in jeopardy. So they supressed the Knights Templar with extreme prejudice and drove the Priory of Sion underground, where for 700 years they survived as a secret society. The Cathars were also guardians of these secrets, and the Albigensian Crusade

(1209–29) was specifically aimed at eliminating this threat to the Papal throne. In subsequent centuries, grand masters such as Leonardo da Vinci (1452–1519) and Isaac Newton (1643–1727) kept the group alive with secret messages hidden in artwork and arcane scientific dialogues.

Then, in the 20th century, Pierre Plantard (1920–2000) stumbled across the story when he found documents secreted in a remote parish church in Rennes-le-Château, near Carcassonne, the old stamping ground of the Cathars. Then ancient documents supporting his story, chronicling the history of the Priory of Sion, were found in the Bibliothèque Nationale.

Plantard wrote several books on the subject and, perhaps not surprisingly, also claimed to be a member of the ancient Merovingian line. But he was not the only one to have money flowing into his coffers; the writer Dan Brown (1964–) pulled together many of the same strands and made millions of dollars.

Sadly, it was all revealed as a hoax in 1993 when Plantard was forced in front of a French court to reveal that he had organized forged documents. It turned out that Plantard was just a common swindler with an overactive imagination and a criminal record. The "historical documents" were the work of the forger Philippe de Chérisey (1923–85), who had smuggled his works into the French National Library. But, as with much bogus history and pseudoscience, individuals remain who are determined to believe in the Priory of Sion, even though the story has now been thoroughly debunked.

ABOVE Isaac Newton was reputed to be a Grand Master of the Priory of Sion. No doubt he was not consulted in the matter.

MOST EXPLOSIVE OF ALL WERE THE WRITINGS OF MARY, DETAILING HER RELATIONSHIP WITH JESUS AND HER JOURNEY TO FRANCE. THESE OFFICIALLY DEBUNKED THE CATHOLIC STORY THAT CHRIST WAS DIVINE AND THE POPES WERE HIS SPIRITUAL REPRESENTATIVES ON EARTH.

CHAPTER 5

MODERN-DAY SECRET SOCIETIES

Even now secret societies have a hold on our imaginations. While it can be presumed that they no longer engage in human sacrifice or devil worship, many remain aloof from most people and are unwilling to share their hidden existence. Are they harmless cranks dressing up in interesting frocks and getting together for a knees-up and a buffet? Or are they secretive power brokers pulling the strings of different governments and faiths around the world?

Ku Klux Klan

The hooded organization that has struck terror into millions of black Americans, been responsible for thousands of brutal lynchings, and become an archetype for a racist terrorist organization began its existence as a good-ol'-boys' drinking club. A relatively harmless gathering developed into a secret society determined to avenge the Confederate defeat in the American Civil War that raged from 1861 to 1865.

As 1864 began, it seemed to the leaders of the Confederacy that there was still a chance they could stop the Union juggernaut and at least obtain international support for the slave state. The American Civil War began in January 1861 when the Southern slave-owning states sought to secede from the United States upon the election of Abraham Lincoln (1809–65), the Republican president elected partly on a platform of abolishing slavery.

It was no "civil" war. Throughout the border states an unrelentingly brutal guerrilla war was waged in which civilians and soldiers alike learned to expect no mercy. It was equally horrific on the battlefield, where new weapons such as long-arm rifles, repeating carbines, and shrapnel shells cut down hundreds of thousands of soldiers. Atrocities abounded and one of the worst occurred when Confederate General Nathan Bedford Forrest with 2,000 mounted Southerners overran Fort Pillow on April 12, 1864. Half of the captured Union garrison consisted of African American soldiers, and Forrest (1821–77), refusing to acknowledge their POW status, massacred them all to a man, his troops bayonetting or shooting them even as they threw down their arms to plead for mercy.

ABOVE **While still revered in the South, the Confederate General Nathan Bedford Forrest may have been responsible for many race-based atrocities.**

But by late 1864 the war turned against the South as Northern resources were marshaled under the brilliant leadership of General Ulysses S. Grant (1822–85). In the western Secessionist states General William Tecumseh Sherman (1820–91) ordered the burning of much of the city of Atlanta before beginning his march to the sea on December 15, 1864. He cut a swathe of destruction 300 miles long and

ABOVE **William Tecumseh Sherman coined the phrase "War is Hell." His destructive march through the south to Savannah fueled lasting resentments.**

60 miles wide before reaching Savannah. "War is Hell," Sherman said famously, and this bloody destructive campaign led to generations of hatred between North and South, which the Klan would feed off in its murderous enterprises.

These and other victories emboldened a re-elected Lincoln to pass through Congress the Thirteenth Amendment to the Constitution, abolishing slavery, on January 31, 1865. By April, the rebel armies were crumbling and on April 9th the last organized army, under General Robert E. Lee (1807–70), surrendered to General Grant at Appomattox Court House.

It Started with Six

The war was won, but many Southerners refused to recognize that they had lost and that African Americans from now on were not to be treated as slaves. On December 25, 1865 in the small rural town of Pulaski in southern Tennessee six ex-Confederate soldiers—John C. Lester, John B. Kennedy, James R. Crowe, Frank McCord, J. Calvin Jones, and Richard Reed—decided to have a bit of a lark and found a secret society. It seems the aims of this society were to get drunk and dress up in outlandish robes. One of the early members was something of a scholar and picked up the Greek word *kuklos*, meaning circle, which combined with "clan" to become the Ku Klux Klan (KKK).

This group of six developed many of the trappings that would later characterize the larger organization—blending mysticism with secret initiation tasks they named their chief officer the Grand Cyclops, and their vice president was designated as the Grand Magi. Where these bizarre names came from is something of a mystery, and it is likely that the initial group was more of a drinking club than anything else.

The original members developed the white mask and tall hat, a gown or robe, and even covers to hide the identity of their horses; this was necessary in the small communities in the South, if one was to maintain anonymity, as the distinctive markings of individual horses were as recognizable as faces. The small group carried on and were surprised to find that local African Americans were terrified of these midnight excursions and soon copycat organizations were springing up all over the South. The robes combined with the human skull and two thigh bones became the badge of recognition.

A solemn oath was sworn by all new members in which they pledged to carry out every order made by any Cyclops or Assistant Cyclops, and that the doom of all traitors should befall them if they failed in this duty.

This wasn't the only white supremacist group to form at this time, but when ex-Confederate generals such as Forrest gave their support to the fledgling organization chapters mushroomed throughout the South. As Northern troops and their supporters moved into positions of government in the Secessionist states, the KKK sought to maintain white dominance within society by burning houses, lynching African Americans, burning churches, and killing Northerners.

So bad was the situation in some states, particularly Mississippi, that large bands of ex-Confederate soldiers roamed at will, causing havoc and destruction. In 1867, the first official national convention was held. This sought to codify and militarize the organization, which its members called The Invisible Empire of the South. Nathan Bedford Forrest became the first Grand Wizard and national head, seeking to bring some unity to the organization. But the chapters remained local affairs where groups elected their own leaders and acted according to their own whims. Grand Dragons became the ruler of each realm (state), and a Grand Titan was responsible for each county, while Grand Cyclops continued to run each "den."

Soon there were tens of thousands of masked horsemen riding through the South. One of their key tasks was to disrupt the 1868 elections, and in Louisiana alone 2,000 citizens were killed or beaten to prevent them registering to vote. In some parishes 100 percent of the vote was Democrat (which was the party seen as more sympathetic to the Klan's policies), Republicans had been jailed before being shot, or else were beaten as they tried to approach voting booths.

ABOVE **Klan robes in a museum. Similar regalia is still worn by those who march with the KKK today.**

All sectors of Southern society were represented: ex-cons, murderers, demobbed soldiers, plantation overseers, Democratic politicians, poor unskilled farm workers—any who felt threatened by the new order took up arms to keep the blacks subservient. Congressman James M. Hinds (1833–68) was assassinated, as were many Republican politicians throughout the South. Small bands rode through the countryside, burning churches, kidnapping community leaders, wiping out families, and destroying economic assets.

By 1869 the scale of atrocities had grown out of control and many crooks and criminals donned the costume whether they were Klan members or not, using the anonymity it bestowed on them to carry out burglaries or violently settle scores. Shocked at the turmoil he had helped unleash, Forrest called for the organization to be disbanded. The Ku Klux Act was passed by Congress in 1871, in which the Klan was declared a terrorist organization; "night riding" was banned; and former General, now President, Grant authorized the use of military force to suppress the disorder. Some Southern counties were placed under martial law, and thousands of members were arrested and given jail terms. Republican militias joined in and retaliated in kind for any KKK atrocities. By 1872, the first KKK was effectively broken.

BELOW The victor of the Civil War, Ulysses S. Grant. He moved decisively against the KKK as president of the United States.

Nevertheless, the attraction of dressing up in funny hats and burning wooden crosses obviously had a deep appeal to many Southerners, and the period after World War One saw a remarkable resurgence of the group and their ideas. No doubt an informal network of supremacists remained among the Southern states, and in 1915 a movie called *The Birth Of a Nation*, directed by D.W. Griffith (1875–1948), portrayed the clan as heroic defenders of white "Aryans."

This movie portrayed Southern whites as being besieged by Republicans and African Americans trying to set up a black empire in the South. The movie also contained the iconography that we now associate with the KKK: the pointed white robes, various crosses and insignia, and, most importantly, the burning cross which Klan members see not as representing the destruction of Christian values, but as symbolic of a light shining in the darkness of a threatening new world.

The KKK Rises Again

It was William J. Simmons (1880–1945), a defrocked minister, who wrote the charter for the resurrected movement. By lighting a huge cross on the top of Stone Mountain, Georgia, Simmons symbolically proclaimed a new attempt to establish white supremacy, Protestant Christianity, nationalism, and the purity of white women in the Southern states.

Perhaps adapting techniques he had seen in *The Birth of a Nation*, Simmons became the chief propagandist for the new movement. Media were invited to KKK bashes, and all the stops were pulled out in an effort to get national attention. The shadowy organization attracted thousands of new adherents. Cult paraphernalia such as white robes, masks, swords, and elaborate initiation ceremonies combined with altars draped in American flags added to the powerful symbolism of the burning cross.

ABOVE **William J. Simmons's use of propaganda, symbolism, and racism was a catalyst for the rebirth of the KKK in the 1920s.**

The reinvigorated clans saw many enemies threatening their values: Jews, Catholics, Asians, communists, Unionists, European migrants, and non-Anglo-Saxon immigrants were all seen as dangerous to white society. The rampant crime generated by Prohibition and the rule of gangsters was also seen as a threat, as were the loose morals of the Jazz Age.

Christian fundamentalist preachers joined the KKK and actively sought recruits. By the 1920s membership was in the millions and the organization had become a national phenomenon, moving into Northern states such as Oklahoma, Pennsylvania, New Jersey, and New York. Their numbers were such that many state and even federal elections were determined by Klan influence. Anti-immigration legislation and immigration quotas satisfied some of the Klan demands, but they persisted in violent attacks on their perceived enemies. However, within this success lay the second Klan's downfall. Having such a broad membership and lacking any meaningful national power structure meant that rabid psychopaths could determine the agenda through acts of violence. D.C. Stephenson (1891–1966), the Grand Dragon of the Indiana Klan, was a particularly nasty piece of work. Initially, he was remarkably successful

ABOVE David Curtiss "Steve" Stephenson (1891–1966) was appointed Grand Dragon (state leader) of the Indiana branch of the Ku Klux Klan in 1923.

as a Klan recruiter and in a few short years nearly half of Indiana's adult males were members. Stephenson wasn't only concerned with "moral" issues. As a politician, he always had his eye on the main game and by controlling initiation protocols and having a monopoly on the sale of Klan costumes and paraphernalia he amassed a tremendous fortune. The power went to Stephenson's head and he presumed that none could touch him.

He was brought down by the vicious rape of a young white literacy worker named Madge Oberholtzer (1896–1925). The young woman was seized by some KKK goons and forced to drink straight whiskey. She was then taken to Stephenson's private train, held captive there for several days, and repeatedly raped. These rapes were incredibly violent and the woman was bitten all over her body. Some bites were particularly deep, especially on her breasts, and these wounds led to infections that contributed to her death in 1925, after she had been released. Tried and found guilty, Stephenson put further nails into the KKK coffin by spilling the beans on the rampant corruption around the Klan and named many politicians who had been paid for their services. Membership began to drop rapidly as the true nature of the organization became clear.

This trend was exacerbated when the Alabama chapter led a wave of beatings and lynchings in 1927. Any who were seen as acting in a way deemed offensive to the Klan's racist credo were attacked, whether they were black or white. This propensity for violence once again removed the KKK from mainstream American values and by the 1930s membership had dropped to about 40,000. Some states passed legislation banning the wearing of masks (except for holiday costumes of fancy dress).

As the media, the federal government, and Northern liberals became aware of the desperate conditions and discrimination suffered by blacks in many Southern states, widespread movements began to emerge aimed at redressing the wrongs inflicted over generations. Freedom rides, massed rallies, and the high profile of civil rights leaders such as Martin Luther King Jr. (1929–68) made it an urgent issue as the North sought

to empower black communities. Fighting these aims was a loose confederation of Klan organizations, including the White Knights of Mississippi. This group was seen as radically violent by other chapters and by 1964 boasted up to 10,000 members and supporters. Bombings, murder, and vandalism were common. It seemed not a day went by when flaming crosses weren't lit at some crossroads or on a hill overlooking the seemingly peaceful rural landscape.

ABOVE **Martin Luther King abhorred the excesses of the resurgent KKK. While it has never been proved, he may have been assassinated on Klan orders.**

While not a huge organization like the early KKK, the third Ku Klux Klan was a more shadowy group composed of like-minded white racists in the police and courts, wealthy businesspeople, and poorer whites who carried out the violent deeds. Years of federal persecution had created a largely underground organization tied together by a hatred of African Americans and a determination to maintain white supremacy. This was all too tangible in many Southern states. Jim Crow laws segregated the black community from the whites: blacks had to sit in the back of buses, could not eat in white sections of restaurants, and were educated in black-only schools. Any black who got "uppity" would be beaten or lynched.

ABOVE The Klan began as something of a good ol' boys' drinking club. By playing on the fears of white Americans, it became an intergenerational phenomenon.

The key weapon utilized by organizations like the White Knights was to dissuade blacks from registering to vote. Unregistered voters could not sit on juries, and of course could not vote for governments or officials sympathetic to their needs. Any individuals who sought to register would be intercepted and beaten, and organizations that encouraged members of their parish to enroll—even churches—would be burned to the ground. In 1964 alone, 36 churches were destroyed.

In 1964, the Freedom Summer began. This involved Northern activists flooding the South with the intention of enrolling as many blacks as possible to vote—in large numbers and in full view of the media. Mississippi would be a particular target, but the White Knights were not going to take this interference lying down.

On June 7, 1964, 300 White Knights held a rally, and their Imperial Wizard, Samuel Bowers (1924–2006), proclaimed that they would fight the "nigger communist" invasion with an armed and violent hit-and-run group. He was as good as his word, and the atrocity that was perpetrated was typical of hundreds of crimes carried out by the third Ku Klux Klan.

Three activists—Andrew Goodman (1943–64), Michael Schwerener (1939–64) and James Earl Chaney (1943–64)—were given the task of organizing enrolment booths for the local blacks in Meridian County, Mississippi. The Klan, led by Bowers and assisted by Exalted Grand Cyclops Frank J. Herndon, began to assemble a party to take out the activists. Their key man was a White Knight "investigator," James T. Harris, who kept tabs on the three men and called in their location so that the lynching party could go to work.

On the morning of June 21, 1964 the three activists inspected the burned-out remains of Mount Zion Methodist Church, one of their chosen locations to set up an enrollment center. Their details were passed to the Neshoba County Sheriff. Soon after, the three were pulled over and locked up in the Neshoba County Jail on trumped-up speeding charges. The time they spent there was used to assemble the Klan's lynching party.

At 10 p.m. the trio were released, but any idea of freedom was short-lived. As they drove out of Meridian County, they were shadowed by the Mississippi Highway Patrol, who radioed the whereabouts of the doomed trio to the Klan. A convoy of pickups and station wagons soon surrounded the activists' car and forced them to pull over onto the darkened Mississippi roads. The locals knew something was up and made sure they stayed home with drawn blinds, determined not to be involved. Schwerener, Chaney, and Goodman were driven to an isolated location and hauled out of their vehicle. Goodman was pushed into a kneeling positon and shot in the head. Schwereners's assassination followed soon after. Chaney was the only African American in the trio, so his end was not so swift. The lynching party beat and tortured him, put a bullet in his guts, and only then finished the job with a head shot.

The Klan's operatives then hauled the bodies to a dam and there concealed them with the use of a grader while the victims' vehicle was torched. An autopsy of Andrew Goodman, showing fragments of red clay in his lungs and grasped in his fists, suggests he was probably buried alive alongside the already dead Chaney and Schwerener.

ABOVE **Most of the symbols that we now associate with the KKK in fact came from the imagination of movie director D. W. Griffith.**

This was only one incident among many. Schoolgirls killed, churches and synagogues firebombed, and activists forced to commit suicide were among some of the atrocities committed. But it was not enough. The FBI was perhaps forced to become active in the area and began to use an extensive network of informers to disrupt KKK activities in their heartland, particularly Georgia and Mississippi. And the full weight of the federal legislature swiftly passed the Civil Rights Act of 1964, the Voting Rights Act of 1965, and the Civil Rights Act of 1968, empowering African American communities and reducing the Klan from a fearsome secret organization to a bunch of wackos out of touch with mainstream America.

There are possibly six to ten thousand members of the Klan currently in America and even they have splintered into White Camelia and several competing organizations going by names such as the Imperial Klans of America and the Knights of the White Camelia. Their association with neo-Nazis has tarred them with the same brush, and now they are seen as an anti-American fringe group.

THE BLACK MAN AS SECOND-CLASS CITIZEN

Until the Civil Rights Movement of the 1960s and 1970s, African Americans were held in a subservient position through lynching and discriminatory laws. Even when membership of the KKK was not too strong, many white citizens were only too happy to be judge, jury, and executioner.

Thousands of blacks were lynched in the Southern states after the Civil War. While many of the killings were Klan-motivated, most were not. The Southern police were often happy to stand by and watch the killings, and many released victims from the sheriffs' lock-ups straight into the hands of the baying mob. Judges often approved of such behavior, not that they were forced to adjudicate in many such cases: it is estimated that less than 1 percent of whites accused of being involved in a lynching were ever brought to trial. All-white juries ensured that even this tiny number got off scot-free.

Only voters were allowed to sit on juries, and one of the key activities of the KKK was to prevent African Americans from signing up to vote. The lack of black participation in the electoral process led to the other, more formal means of keeping them in the position of second-class citizens.

In the 1890s, the US Supreme Court legislated that segregation of the races was legal. The states of Alabama, Florida, Georgia, Louisiana, Mississippi, and North and South Carolina jumped on this legislative bandwagon and passed multiple laws restricting the rights of their black citizens. They were banned from associating with whites in many venues, including buses, restaurants, pools, and public conveniences. These so-called Jim Crow laws show that racism ran deep in many Southern states and that the KKK was only an outward manifestation of this prejudice.

RIGHT Civil rights activists protesting racial inequality in the 1960s. They faced violence, intimidation, and even lynching at the hands of white supremacists.

SKULL AND BONES

Skull and Bones has all the trappings of a secret society. Its lodge is a mighty stone edifice as inscrutable as an Easter Island statue. Though located in the heart of Yale University, with a membership of prominent Americans, little is known of what goes on behind the lodge's walls. Members call it "The Tomb."

In fact, Skull and Bones is basically like a drunken fraternity with rules that might just as well be found in a *Boy's Own* adventure book. Its importance comes from its location in the heart of America's old money and old boy networks.

Skull and Bones is actually a fraternity house. Just like in a John Belushi (1949–82) movie, frat houses are scenes of mischief and trouble, and this upper-class fraternity is not so different. Every year 15 members of the Yale community, from the wealthiest or most powerful families, get a tap on the shoulder to say that they have been offered a spot.

BELOW "The Tomb" at Yale University is the headquarters of the Skull and Bones. What goes on behind these forbidding walls is still a mystery.

The society was founded in 1832 by William Huntington Russell (1809–85), whose family money, unsurprisingly for the time, came from trading slaves and opium. Surely many later

inductees might balk at an organization with such a founder, but apparently not. The co-founder was Alphonso Taft (1810–91), father of the 27th American President, William Howard Taft (1857–1930).

The early members gave the club many other names including the Order of Death, the Order, the Eulogian Club, and Lodge 322. Initiated members refer to themselves by a number of titles including Bonesmen, Knights of Eulogia, and the Boodle Boys. Women have only recently been allowed to join, and with a logic it is hard to fault are called Boneswomen, Ladies of Eulogia, or Boodle Girls.

However, despite the fact that women can be admitted, it is still a frat house with a healthy dose of American testosterone-filled fun and games. When a junior is invited to join, they are given a formal initiation in the form of a scroll. It is tied with a black ribbon which is fixed in place with a black wax seal. On the seal is a skull and crossbones, and below this symbol the number 322.

To be tapped for membership is seen as a great honor, although occasionally some refuse. The initiation process is quite rigorous and, unsurprisingly, since the proceedings were invented by young men, it is quite sexual in nature. Novices meet weekly for at least a year indulging in self-analysis and critique. On their first day, they are given a name, with figures from arcane mythology being popular, including Boaz, Magog (for the man with the best record with women), Gog (for virgins), Little Devil (for the vertically challenged), and Long Devil (for the tallest).

Being an elite organization, they dine off Hitler's china set, captured after World War Two. They are encouraged to refer to themselves as knights and all outsiders as barbarians. All clocks within the Tomb run five minutes fast, as a token of their superiority.

As part of the bonding service, new members must give detailed accounts of their lives, with especial attention given to the "C.B. statement." This Connubial Bliss statement has to be a warts-and-all recitation of their sexual experiences. An inductee must earn the cohort's trust by detailing failures as well as successes in the bedroom. Not only does this bind them together, but it means that if ever a member should break the rules of the frat house, there will be blackmailing payback.

The C.B. statement is related while lying naked in an open sarcophagus. (You would hope they have central heating!) This is followed by naked mud wrestling and assorted hijinks. Like many similar organizations, challenges are set for the inductee to perform in order to gain full membership. As the name Skull and Bones suggests, many of these involve getting hold of body parts and even grave robbing. George "Dubya" Bush's grandad was apparently quite a wild boy during his freshman years. Prescott Bush (1895–1972) decided to do his bit for the interior decoration of the Skull and Bones Tomb. He and some fellows dug up and grabbed the skull of the legendary Apache resistance fighter Geronimo (1829–1909) from its resting place at the federal cemetery at Fort Sill, Oklahoma. Apparently, if you believe the story, it sits with pride of place in the main hall, known as the Skull and Bones room.

An inductee must understand that they are committed to lifelong secrecy about the order. If any member is in a room and the order is mentioned or a question is asked, the "knight" is required to immediately leave the conversation and the room as a guarantee that they won't spill the beans or let anything slip.

When the 15 yearly inductees are finally made full members, each is given a grandfather clock and a $15,000 cash gift. A photo of the cohort is taken with all sitting or standing proudly beside a table on which sits a skull and crossbones, with a grandfather clock behind them. The clock is always set at 8 p.m.

This commitment to secrecy means there is very little known about what goes on behind the closed doors of the Tomb. There are rumors of banquets being held in rooms bedecked with skulls. As well as Geronimo's, they apparently possess the skulls of Pancho Villa (1878–1923) and Che Guevara (1928–67). Some say that good wine is quaffed out of those very same skulls. In the bowels of the building are temple spaces, perhaps outfitted for pagan worship or possibly covered with signs of the Illuminati.

What is known is that Skull and Bones is a very powerful and privileged order. Not many secret societies can boast their own island or summer retreat surrounded by acres of parkland. The venue in question is Deer Island, located in the St. Lawrence River between the United States and Canada. It boasts two tennis courts, a boathouse, luxurious accommodation, and an amphitheater.

The offspring of several American families that have been at the heart of the financial and political establishment for generations—including the Cheneys, the Bushes, the Tafts, the Walkers, and the Clarks—have also been members of Skull and Bones. No doubt intermarriage amongst them and the swapping of favors help them stay there.

In 2004, the Democrat John Kerry (1943–) ran against incumbent George W. Bush (1946–) for the US presidency, but both men are members of Skull and Bones. Eleven of Bush's first administration were Skull and Bones members. This certainly proves that while they might have a monopoly on wealth and power, they do not have a monopoly on brains. Perhaps the troubles plaguing the world at the present moment wouldn't have come to pass if different people had been holding the reins in those crucial years.

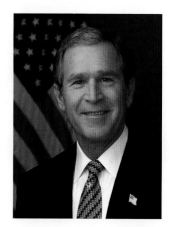

BELOW George W. Bush and his political opponent John Kerry are both members of the Skull and Bones. The society is a bastion of American privilege.

THE RAELIANS

While the activities of many of the secret societies and cults within this book make for pretty grim reading, there is perhaps one society that could be fun to join—the Raelians. They have a largely positive worldview, but within the inner sanctum there is a great deal of secrecy as they work toward cloning and other "alien" technologies.

This group was founded by the French writer, musician, and race car driver Claude Vorilhon (1946–) in 1974. He felt he'd been summoned to take a walk in the crater of an extinct volcano in the Auvergne region of France. Claude tells of how he felt guilty and that he should have been at work rather than traipsing around the countryside. Nevertheless, some force drew him there, and his questions were soon answered when he saw a bright flashing light in the sky. Soon the flashing light became more intense and descending from the heavens was a bell-shaped silver craft. Claude was initially a bit nervous but was also excited at the same time. "This is one of those UFOs I've been hearing about," he thought. The craft was about 23 feet (7 meters) wide and landed on three spindly legs near to where Claude was

BELOW **Claude Vorilhon claims he was visited by aliens, who instructed him to have sex with as many people as possible.**

standing. Emerging from a trapdoor below the craft was a concertina staircase. Quite nervous by now, Claude decided that if he saw any weapons he would run away, but until then he would give the strange visitors the benefit of the doubt.

It is lucky he did, as soon a little four-foot (1.2 meter) man emerged from the craft. Dressed in a green tunic and with a goatee beard and long hair, the overwhelming vibe this intergalactic visitor gave off was one of love. This extraterrestrial, who named himself Yahweh, spoke to the stunned Frenchman and declared that Claude now had a new role—he was to be the human ambassador for the race of Elohim. Claude would also change his name to Raël. For the next six days Vorilhon was closeted in the spacecraft with the little visitor and given the truth about humanity's origins.

BELOW **A Raelian member dressed as an alien in South Korea. The society continues to preach a strong anti-nuclear message.**

The core message was that he was to spread the word of Raël, which translates as "Light of God." Elohim was the original word for a divine being, which had been corrupted to "God." Therefore, Raël means, "The Light of God/Elohim."

Yahweh explained to Claude that he was an Eloha and that his race—plural Elohim—lived in a galaxy far away. For many years top Elohim scientists had been creating life through cloning techniques, but when some of the Elohim became suspicious, the scientists were forced to find a new planet to continue their experiments. So 25,000 years ago they set out from their home planet and discovered Earth which was just a big ball of water. By using atomic weapons, the Elohim blew out holes which became oceans and raised up land masses which became continents.

From here they began to create life. Starting with viruses and bacteria they soon progressed to simple plants, fish, reptiles, and finally the crowning glory of mammals. The entire fossil record, claimed the little green man, was a result of his people's experimentation and every living creature was fine-tuned to fit within its environment. The laboratory for this "intelligent design" was an artificial continent called the Garden of Eden.

Eventually it was decided to use Eloha DNA and create humans. The purest forms of humans with the greatest amount of Eloha DNA were of course the Israelites, and it was the country of Israel where the Elohim would next visit.

ABOVE Raelians demonstrate in South Korea. Some governments fear the movement, even though Raelians believe in brotherly love and peace.

Throughout history, this wise little green man continued, the Elohim had sent messengers to make sure that humans stayed in touch with their creators. Some of these messengers were of course Buddha, Jesus, Muhammad, founder of Mormonism Joseph Smith (1805–44), John the Baptist, and Moses. Art throughout the ages was full of images of Elohim, with angels and cherubs being examples.

Yahweh also explained how the new Raelian religion should work once the basis of intelligent design had been passed to the newly anointed prophet. Firstly, there is no God. The creators are the Elohim, and since we are genetically related to them we are in fact the creators. Eternal life will be provided by believers through cloning. Since there is no God, any behavior that is frowned on by the major religions is permissible if it makes you feel good and doesn't hurt others. Claude Vorilhon emphasized this message, and many of his writings and manuals of the society say that sex is encouraged by the Elohim.

In fact, by his own account on several occasions Raël, as Claude became known, was transported to the Elohim home world where he was involved in extended "bathing sessions" with six genetically perfect women, all of whom were perfect examples of their race on earth including Nordic, Asian, and African genotypes.

This aspect of the society may be one of the main attractions of the cult to its followers (compared to a belief in little green men). Homosexuality, bisexuality, pansexuality, and masturbation are all actively encouraged, as any puritanical prohibitions are just corruptions of the original messages left by earlier prophets. Consensual sexual activity between adults is promoted as a health-giving practice. This society basically says, "it is good to get your gear off!" The practice of "sensual meditation" is the best way to reach the divine, while other aspects of the society are pretty casual and no punishments are given for those who don't pay tithes or regularly attend sessions.

In a perfect world, as envisaged by the Raelians, the globe will be divided into 12 regions and people can go to whichever region they want. These regions will not need weapons, as no wars will be fought and all will be ruled by a "geniocracy," where only the most intelligent will be able to vote or rule. All personal possessions will be communally owned and strict birth control will radically reduce the size of the population.

According to the society's writings, their role is to prepare a flying saucer pad in Israel, which will welcome the Elohim when they descend from the sky and bring in a new era of peace and harmony. Our society will be elevated to an intergalactic technological society of peace and harmony.

The Raelians' headquarters is based in Switzerland, and the activities here are kept secret from the general public. It appears that the upper hierarchy, led of course by Claude Vorilhon as the "guide of guides," has spent millions of dollars on the science of cloning. A subsidiary is the secretive **organization** called Clonaid, which

ACCORDING TO THE SOCIETY'S WRITINGS, THEIR ROLE IS TO PREPARE A FLYING SAUCER PAD IN ISRAEL, WHICH WILL WELCOME THE ELOHIM WHEN THEY DESCEND FROM THE SKY AND BRING IN A NEW ERA OF PEACE AND HARMONY.

in 2002 claimed it had birthed the first successfully cloned human. Since then a minimum of 12 more clones have been born. Many of those who contribute funds to the Raelians do so with the belief that as they are infertile they may be able to obtain a clone of themselves. The society has so far refused to hand over any of these offspring for genetic testing, citing the fear that the children may be removed from their "parents." Most respected experts in the field maintain that successful cloning of humans is not yet possible and that the group will not submit to scientific testing as it is just a money-making fraud. The more outlandish claims they have made include the ability to transfer a person's mind into a cloned copy of themselves, thereby guaranteeing immortality.

ABOVE Members of the Raelian cult march in a street parade in Montreal, Canada. Members are encouraged to get their gear off whenever possible.

THE KNIGHTS OF THE GOLDEN CIRCLE

The Knights of the Golden Circle was a secret society founded in Cincinnati, Ohio, on July 4th, 1854 by an adventurer named George W.L. Bickley (1819–67). Bickley was known as a quack and a charlatan but he did have one idea that attracted a great deal of support, especially in Texas. Bickley founded the Knights of the Golden Circle with the intention of establishing a slaveholding empire that would cover hundreds of thousands of square miles, with Havana, Cuba, at its center. Other territories to be included in this slavocracy were Texas, Mexico, the West Indies, all of Central America, and part of South America.

The organization soon had several thousand "knights" (members) divided into several hundred "castles" (lodges). In 1858, they merged with the expansionist Order of the Lone Star, which had almost 15,000 members, and plans were soon afoot to raise a private army and invade Mexico. In 1860 several thousand knights gathered in Texas to launch an attack across the border, but a lack of funds soon led to the project being abandoned.

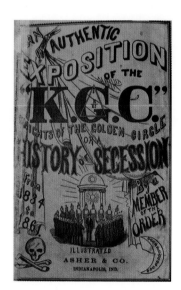

Nevertheless, the movement continued to grow, a new headquarters was established in Washington, D.C., and the organization began to publish its own newspaper. Many articles promoted secession from the Union, and by the time Abraham Lincoln was elected the knights had begun organizing Southern militias to resist what they regarded as potential Northern aggression. The knights also persecuted Unionists who were living in the Southern states and held pro-secession rallies. They planned to take over federal forts in North Carolina and Virginia, and there is evidence that some members planned to assassinate Abraham Lincoln in 1861, as he passed through Baltimore on the way to his inauguration.

ABOVE **A propaganda pamphlet from the Knights of the Golden Circle. Thankfully the society and its racist agenda did not survive beyond the American Civil War.**

Once the civil war began, those Knights of the Golden Circle who remained in the Union states led the Copperheads, a loose grouping of Democrats who sought an immediate end to the conflict and a peaceful resolution with the slave-owning states.

The Northern press made much of the power of the Knights of the Golden Circle and whipped up paranoid hysteria with reports of thousands of knights ready to emerge and seize power in states such as Indiana. There were, it was reported, dedicated hit squads of fanatical knights preparing to launch incendiary and bombing campaigns in New York, Boston, and Philadelphia.

A pamphlet was circulated entitled "A True Disclosure and Exposition of the Knights of the Golden Circle, including the Secret Signs, Grips and Charges of the third Degree as Practiced by the Order," indicating that the order had a membership as numerous and powerful as the Freemasons.

It turned out that the conspiracy amounted to nought. Although some members of the Knights of the Golden Circle were successful in leading some raids and incursions into federal territory, few, if any, in the top echelons of the Confederate Army were members. As the war turned against the Southern states, the organization renamed itself the Order of American Knights. The Confederate government funneled large amounts of much-needed bullion and arms to the Copperheads in anticipation of widespread uprisings against Lincoln's government, but nothing eventuated from these grand schemes.

Even before this, Bickley had been captured by the Union Army after he deserted from the Confederates. He had put in a short stint as an army surgeon but, not liking the work, he had fled only to be captured. Rather than a mastermind and grand master, he proved to be a petty thief and bigamist and by 1864 it was widely acknowledged that the Knights of the Golden Circle were defunct.

Some rumors persist, however. It is possible that John Wilkes Booth (1838–65) was funded and armed by the group for his assassination of Lincoln and that a network of knights helped him flee. There are also reports of "Golden Circle" caches of bullion still hidden in the sands of Texas.

RIGHT **John Wilkes Booth may have been a member of the Knights of the Golden Circle. He did the South no favors by assassinating Lincoln.**

THE CAMBRIDGE APOSTLES

At first glance, this might seem to be a benign secret society dedicated to eating whales (sardines on toast) and discussing a bit of literature and philosophy. But like all secret societies it harbors some dark secrets—in this case, helping to create the network behind one of the greatest spy scandals of the 20th century.

The Apostles is a secret society made up of members of Cambridge University in the UK. Most of those selected come from the colleges of St. John's, Trinity, and King's. It is largely a discussion or debating group that focuses on topics such as ethics, literature, and divinity. It was founded in 1820 by George Tomlinson (1794–1863) with the original title the Cambridge Conversazione Society. There were 12 original members, which inevitably led to the club calling itself the Cambridge Apostles. Of course, being a secret society mainly made up of undergraduates, they are termed apostles, while members who have left the university are known as angels. Every two years or so all of the angels and apostles get together at a gala dinner to celebrate their exclusive membership.

BELOW King's College Cambridge was the heart of the Cambridge Apostles. Whether they still meet is something of a mystery.

No one could apply to join the Apostles. He or, after 1970, she would be proposed by a member, and all of the other members

would have to vote to accept the submission. The decision needed to be unanimous and the nominated individual would have to be recognized for having a unique talent in some field. The past and present membership includes some brilliant individuals. John Maynard Keynes (1883–1946), the noted economic philosopher; the poet Rupert Brooke (1887–1915); Erasmus Darwin (1804–81), brother of Charles (1809–82); Poet Laureate Alfred Lord Tennyson (1809–92); Prime Minister Arthur Balfour (1848–1930); and the influential Victor Rothschild, the 3rd Baron Rothschild (1910–90), were all members of the club. Some of the leading lights of the Bloomsbury Group, including Leonard Woolf (1880–1969)— husband of Virginia Woolf (1882–1941)—and Lytton Strachey (1880–1932), were also members.

As with many secret societies there was a mysterious language known only to the members. An undergraduate who was nominated for induction was known as an "embryo" and his nominator was the "father." The induction ceremony was called the "birth," and when members left the university they "took wing."

ABOVE **Prime Minister Arthur Balfour (1848–1930) was one of the many influential individuals who was a lifelong member of the Cambridge Apostles.**

Once the nomination had been accepted, the "embryo" would be invited to a meeting and told of his good fortune. He would then be briefed on the society's practices, rules, and traditions, and at the same time be sworn to secrecy. He would then sign "The Book," a leatherbound record of all members going back to the 1820s. It also set out a series of rules and suggested punishments for those who didn't rigorously attend all meetings.

Once initiated the member was required to attend regular Saturday evening discussions in one of the members' college rooms. Lots had earlier been drawn to see who would deliver a paper, which would then act as a springboard for the other members to debate and discuss the topic. While thus engaged they would have a 'riot of a time' consuming sardines and coffee. The papers and manuscript notes were stored in "The Book," of which there grew to be more than one volume; all of them were stored in a chest made from Lebanese cedar, known as "the Ark," built in 1886 and currently stored in the Archive Centre Reading Room in King's College.

During the 19th century, it seems that the Cambridge Apostles were progressive liberals who sought to free intellectuals from preconceived ideas and prejudices. They

ABOVE **In the 1930s the Cambridge Apostles began to adopt a leftist ideology. Guy Burgess used his connections to further his career as a Soviet spy.**

also were quite powerful in British society, 34 angels having served in the British Parliament (and even one elected to the US Congress).

By the beginning of the 20th century it is likely that new trends had emerged, as most members were part of a homosexual subculture at the university, and by the 1930s almost all the newer members subscribed to communist ideals. This led to the greatest scandal to befall the secret society, bringing them to public attention for the first time, when in 1951 the Cambridge Spy Ring was broken. Three Apostles—Guy Burgess (1911–63), Donald Maclean (1913–83), and later Kim Philby (1912–88)—were found to be exploiting their public positions in the British government and security services to pass secrets to the Russians. Decades later it was discovered that another member of the society, Anthony Blunt (1907–83), was also a member of the ring. Blunt also recruited many influential Americans and fellow Brits to the Soviet cause. Leo Long and John Peter Astbury were two other Apostles drawn into the web of espionage, and they, too, delivered confidential material to their handlers. The fear of being exposed as a homosexual may have been a reason, along with political ideals, that made many turn against their country.

Victor Rothschild may also have been involved in the conspiracy, although he managed to deflect suspicion and remained privy to many government decisions. It seems he may have gotten off lightly. In 1940, he recruited Anthony Blunt to the secret service. He also rented a house to his good friend Guy Burgess for a peppercorn rent, and worked with the other main actor in the spy ring, Kim Philby, at the MI6 offices based at his Paris mansion. He also admitted to being "sympathetic" to communism.

The Cambridge Apostles may still exist, but nobody is quite sure. Maybe the bad press of the fifties and sixties turned them into a truly secret society, after all.

THE BILDERBERG CONFERENCE

A little-known governor of a small state in the United States of America was invited to attend the 1991 Bilderberg conference. One year later Bill Clinton had risen from his position as Governor of Arkansas to be US President.

Tony Blair was sitting on the opposition benches in the House of Commons in London when he was invited to attend the 1993 Bilderberg conference. In 1994, he was promoted to leadership of the British Labour Party. In May 1997, he was elected prime minister and lasted in that role for 10 years.

Coincidence?

Representatives of the world's largest petroleum companies and automobile manufacturers are regularly invited. Despite the well-attested dangers of fossil fuels and the environmental damage caused by the internal combustion engine, these outdated technologies continue to be the main form of energy generation and transport despite the advantages of carbon-neutral devices.

BELOW Bill Clinton might have owed his election as President of the United States to patronage from powerful members of the Bilderberg conference.

Coincidence? Maybe; maybe not. These are just some of the questions that can be asked about this unique modern secret society.

The Bilderberg conference is just a semi-formal group of "guys" (they are mostly guys) who get together to discuss stuff. There's no conspiracy here. They are not the "new world order," a supranational organization that pulls the strings of all that happens in our world.

That is what the Bilderberg Group would have us believe. In fact, it is a super-secret organization of the world's most powerful people who cloak their actions, meetings, and discussions with an impenetrable veil of silence. Maybe they are up to something nefarious and dark. Maybe not. We simply do not know, as no records are kept and all who attend are sworn to secrecy. This high degree of secrecy has of course led to much speculation as to what they actually get up to in these meetings.

The Bilderberg forum is a three-day meeting that happens once a year at select locations in the developed world. Attendees are allowed on an

invite-only basis, and experts in certain fields may be invited to contribute for one day only. The inaugural meeting was held from May 29 to 31, 1954, in the Hotel de Bilderberg in the pleasant town of Oosterbeek in the Netherlands. It was originally a forum to discuss issues arising from the threat posed by Soviet countries and a means to tie Western Europe and the United States closer together. The first conference was attended by 50 powerful government and business leaders from 11 European nations as well as 11 Americans. President Eisenhower (1890–1969) and the head of the CIA gave this first meeting their blessing and sent high-powered representatives to further American interests. The American government was the biggest sponsor for this inaugural meeting.

This first forum was such a success that a similar meeting has been held every year. A permanent steering committee with a permanent secretary was established and still operates out of the Netherlands. The committee is made up of two representatives from approximately 18 powerful Western countries. It is responsible for issuing invitations, booking an appropriately secure venue for the gathering, and issuing annual conference reports to current and past attendees. Perhaps most importantly, it maintains the contact details of individuals so that they can consult with each other beyond the confines of the conference—perhaps the ultimate old-boys' network. There is a separate advisory group which acts as a "talent-spotting" outfit to identify new inductees.

BELOW Prince Bernhard of the Netherlands. The Bilderberg conference was his brainchild, making him one of the most influential individuals of the 20th century.

Who is the "talent" being invited to Bilderberg? The bodies represented reveal the interests being served. Companies that sponsor or send high-powered executives to attend the forum include Ford, the US Central Intelligence Agency, MI6, British Petroleum, HSBC, Deutsche Bank, Goldman Sachs, Harvard University, Princeton University, Barclays Bank, Fiat automobiles, GlaxoSmithKline, Heinz, Nokia, Xerox, Ryanair, AXA Insurance, the International Monetary Fund, the European Central Bank, Bayer, Chrysler, Airbus, Google, SAAB, Boeing, the US Army, and Shell Oil. There are, it seems, no progressive thinktanks to be seen. The other participants are usually from government organizations, although not many of these are involved in charity.

But from the start, Bilderberg, which after all was the brainchild of Prince Bernhard of the Netherlands (1911–2004), has also mixed new money with old. Henri de Castries (1954–), a French count, and Sir John Sawers (1955–) are example attendees.

De Castries was the chairman of the 2016 conference and comes from aristocratic stock dating back to the Crusades of the Middle Ages, when his family was involved in Holy War against the Muslims. As the count of Castries in rural Anjou, his father was engaged in fighting communists in Indochina and Korea. De Castries himself was a key player on the French right at the heart of the privatization drive of prime minister (later to be president) Jacques Chirac (1932–) in the 1980s, after which he served as chairman and chief executive of insurance giant AXA.

ABOVE The Bilderberg Hotel, after which the conference is named. The first conference was sponsored by the American CIA.

Sawers was the former head of the secret intelligence service MI6 between 2009 and 2014 and before that was political director of the British Foreign Office from 2003 to 2007, after being an advisor to Blair and consulting on the invasion of Iraq.

At its heart the group would appear to be dominated by big business, Western security agencies, and banking. The aim of the meetings appears to be to foster discussions with several key aims—to predict future trends, to avoid conflicts that can affect the bottom line, and perhaps to ensure that maximum profits are maintained by all concerned. Quite often historians, futurists, and statisticians with the expertise to predict trends and likely outcomes are invited to present to the forum.

The delegates no doubt welcome the chance to speak plainly without any press to interrupt or report on their innermost thoughts and blow them up into politically correct controversies. Chatham House rules are followed, where participants can utilize information but not relay the source. No minutes are taken, no resolutions are proposed, no votes are held, no press conferences are given, there are no opening or closing statements, participants are asked not to report on discussions, and no policies are issued.

Attendees avoid the media, and many protesters or reporters that get too close are swiftly arrested and carted off to the local lockup, or at least removed from the scene.

Nevertheless, there must be some purpose to these conferences. Wealthy industrialists and powerful government figures don't fly thousands of miles and stump up thousands of dollars for a harmless chinwag. No doubt some agenda is pursued.

Is the agenda for the benefit of the average Joe in the street? I wouldn't bet on it.

When the Good Turn Bad: The Origins of Organized Crime

Names like the Yakuza, the Mafia, the Triads, and the Tongs strike terror into the hearts of law-abiding citizens in those countries where people are afflicted by such groups. These are secret societies with complex rituals and initiation procedures that place loyalty to the group above all other considerations. This secrecy is now used to protect their criminal endeavors.

All of these groups began as societies that protected the weak rather than exploiting them.

The Mafia

BELOW **Frank Costello, head of the Luciano crime family, testifying before the US government. Few have been able to break the Mafia's code of silence.**

The Mafia began as a brotherhood based in southern Italy and Sicily. For hundreds of years this region had been invaded and plundered by rival powers—Byzantines, Normans, Germans, Muslims, French, Spaniards—all of whom had sought to conquer these strategically important lands. Barons cruelly exploited their hereditary estates and especially their poor tenant peasants.

Often the only way peasants could survive was to band together into armed groups that would use stealth and secrecy to fight injustice. These bands coalesced into alternative power structures that used an omertà, a code of silence, to survive. Soon these "mafia" began to exploit those they had once sought to help protect, demanding protection money and dominating the local economies.

During the 20th century, migrants from the Italian regions of Sicily, Calabria, and Naples established mafia networks throughout the world, especially in America.

ABOVE **Even the FBI could not get someone to inform on Al Capone. He was only put away due to tax dodges.**

The best-known Mafia clans

Cosa Nostra, roughly translated as "this thing of ours." Their home is in Sicily, south of the Italian mainland.

N'drangheta, which translates as "honored society." This group originated in the once-lush region of Calabria, in southern Italy.

Camorra, the third largest Italian Mafia group, originating in Naples, where they still dominate the European fashion trade.

ABOVE Hanafuda cards. A hand of 20 points was the worst possible combination—*yakuza*. Organized criminals took this term as their title, meaning "bad hands."

The Tongs

The Tongs began life in Chinatowns in the big cities of the United States during the 19th century. They began as benevolent societies, meeting secretively in halls (*tong* is the Chinese word for "hall"). Here they swore elaborate promises of secrecy and loyalty. Members contributed regularly to establish funds to help out with funeral costs, medical treatment, and unemployment insurance. They also gave physical protection against other violent and often racist organizations. Soon the Tongs used their numbers to take over illegal rackets such as gambling, opium, and prostitution. Different Tongs fought for supremacy, and by the early 20th century, "tong wars" frequently broke out, with razor-sharp Chinese meat cleavers as the weapon of choice.

The Triads

These organizations began in China to protect the native Han majority from the depredations of ruthless foreigners. They got their name from a group of 133 warrior monks who banded together in 1644 to fight off the Manchu invaders. Most were killed, and five survivors formed the Society of the Heaven and Earth (Tiandihui). They took as their symbol a triangle representing the holy link between heaven, earth, and man—hence the name "triad."

THEY SWORE ELABORATE PROMISES OF SECRECY AND LOYALTY. MEMBERS CONTRIBUTED REGULARLY TO ESTABLISH FUNDS TO HELP OUT WITH FUNERAL COSTS, MEDICAL TREATMENT, AND UNEMPLOYMENT INSURANCE.

Similar and related organizations sprung up throughout China. All carried on with great secrecy lest the Manchu invaders arrest and torture any members. While they claimed to be nationalist organizations, they were essentially criminal organizations that exploited the Chinese love of opium, gambling, and women.

ABOVE **An early photograph depicting Yakuza tattoos. While clothed, they would be able to move undetected through Japanese society.**

One of the best-known Triads was Big-Eared Du's Green Gang. In 1927, Du Yuesheng (1888–1951), to give him his real name, colluded with Chiang Kai-shek (1887–1975) to wipe out all the communists in Shanghai, helping to establish the nationalist government. But with the communist takeover in 1949, the Triads were ruthlessly suppressed, and only those in Hong Kong and Taiwan managed to survive.

The Yakuza

The samurai warrior class liked to see themselves as honorable warriors. In practice samurai were vicious freebooters, massacring political opponents and their subjects with abandon, plundering peasant smallholdings, laying waste and burning crops, and generally slaughtering any who sought to defy them.

A citizen militia was formed to protect peasants. The machi-yokko stockpiled captured weapons and fought off marauding bands of samurai, in some cases ruthlessly pursuing them with long pole weapons called yari.

Then, during the Meiji restoration in the late 19th century, Japan embarked upon a program of modernization, as a result of which the samurai were destroyed as a class. But the less formal machi-yokko survived these reforms and began to refer to themselves as the Yakuza. During their downtime the members gambled, one of their favorite games being hanafuda (flower cards). Involving three cards, the worst hand totalled 20 points, and the worst combination was yakuza: Ya for 8, Ku for 9, and Sa for 3. From protectors of the poor, now they viewed themselves as "the bad hand" or rotten eggs of society.

Recognizable signs for the Yakuza were elaborate tattoos and in some instances severed joints from their pinkie fingers: a yakuza who had somehow transgressed the organization's code was required to hack off the end of his digit as a visible penance. Known as *yubizeum*, the act of cutting off the joint was done in public in front of the appropriate crime boss, symbolizing both the member's error and his courage.

At their high point Yakuza numbers reached 184,000, divided into 5,200 gangs, each with its own territory and rackets. They are still a powerful force within Japanese society.

LEFT **A woodcut of a Ronin, or master-less samurai. It was against men like these that organizations such as the Yakuza were originally formed.**

RECOGNIZABLE SIGNS FOR THE YAKUZA WERE ELABORATE TATTOOS AND IN SOME INSTANCES SEVERED JOINTS FROM THEIR PINKIE FINGERS: A YAKUZA WHO HAD SOMEHOW TRANSGRESSED THE ORGANIZATION'S CODE WAS REQUIRED TO HACK OFF THE END OF HIS DIGIT AS A VISIBLE PENANCE.

HERMETIC ORDER OF THE GOLDEN DAWN

This secret society could be described as the department store of mysticism. It was founded in London in 1888 and offered any and all mystical practices and beliefs to its adherents. Three men are acknowledged as the founders: Dr. William Woodman (1828–91), Dr. William Wynn Westcott (1848–1925), and Samuel Liddell Mathers (1854–1918).

The three gents took their inspiration from the structure of Masonic lodges, although women were made welcome from the outset. The rituals of the order were derived from *The Cipher Manuscripts*, which took a whole lot of spiritual gobbledygook and made it even more arcane by writing it in the remarkably complex Trithemius cipher.

Like all such secret societies the members of the Golden Dawn had to progress through several layers to attain knowledge and understanding. The things that this order offered were very far-ranging (and very far-fetched). Upon passing through all three stages the members would become adept at the following skills: spell casting, the tarot, yoga, astrology, channeling, astral travel, hermeticism (don't ask), alchemy, grimoires (magic texts), geomancy, Hermetic Qabalah, and an understanding of the Ancient Egyptian worship of Isis and Osiris.

One of the best-known members of the Hermetic Order of the Golden Dawn was the infamous occultist Aleister Crowley (1875–1947). But the order wasn't extreme enough for him, and after falling out with most of its members he left and established the Thelema Club, which had the motto, "Do what thou wilt." As for the Hermetic Order of the Golden Dawn, their motto may as well have been, "Believe what thou wilt." It seems that Crowley was told to leave the Hermetic Order of the Golden Dawn due to his inability to hide his sexual proclivity for young men. Crowley went on to live a life of intrigue and mysticism and at one stage even identified himself as the Beast 666 from the Book of Revelation. Even though his sojourn in the Hermetic Order of the Golden Dawn was quite brief it did give him a solid grounding in occult practices that he would later use in his neverending quest for notoriety.

RIGHT **William Westcott founded the Hermetic Order of the Golden Dawn. He grabbed any mystical claptrap he could find and founded a religion.**

SUPER CHRISTIANS OPUS DEI (THE WORK OF GOD)

This secret society of super Christians was founded in 1928 by Josemaría Escrivá in Spain. Opus Dei has not always received good press. In the Hollywood adaptation of Dan Brown's *The Da Vinci Code*, the organization was portrayed as the papal hit squad with Brother Silas employed to do the Vatican's wetwork. While the psychotic albino martial arts expert was a great screen creation, he was also something of an exaggeration.

Nevertheless, in many ways Opus Dei can be seen as a secretive society carrying out a radical Catholic agenda. Members are sworn to spend every minute of the day thinking Christian thoughts and living a life of strict regimentation. Seventy percent of the cult are what are known as supernumeraries, who go about their business in the real world. Numerary members are celibate and live in Opus Dei centers, while approximately 2 percent of the membership are anointed priests.

Once someone is sworn into the society, there are very few personal freedoms even for the supernumeraries. A large portion of their income is garnished while the numerary members pay all of their income to the organization. All members are required to spend much of the day in prayer, and as soon as they wake up their first thought must be *serviam* – Latin for "I will serve." Members are told what books they can read, what movies are appropriate, what to wear, and what to eat. Their mail is strictly censored, and they must confess weekly to a spiritual superior—not only their own spiritual transgressions but also those of other members. Punishments are harsh. Self-flagellation with a cilice, or spiked chain, is common, as is the removal of comforts such as bedding while sleeping.

There are perhaps 100,000 active members at present, but it is impossible to be sure as membership lists are held in secret by the Papacy. Members are often urged to renounce their families in order to get closer to God, and any activity or action must be seen as an attempt to become an "ordinary saint" or someone without sin.

LEFT **Josemaría Escrivá, the founder of Opus Dei. He is still revered as a warrior for Christ.**

FURTHER READING

Books

Begg, Paul and Fido, Martin. *Great Crimes and Trials of the Twentieth Century*. London, Carlton, 1997.

Brackett, D. W. *Holy Terror: Armageddon in Tokyo*. Boulder, CA, Weatherhill, 1996.

Bugliosi, Vincent. *Helter Skelter: The True Story of the Manson Murders*. London, Arrow, 1992.

Clarke, Phil, Hardy, Liz and Williams, Anne. *Executioners: Men and Women Who Kill for the People*. London, Futura, 2008.

Gardiner, Philip. *Secret Societies: Gardiner's Forbidden Knowledge*. London, New Page Books, 2007.

Goldwag, Arthur. *Cults, Conspiracies and Secret Societies*. London, Vintage Books, 2017.

Hieronimus, Robert. *Founding Fathers Secret Societies*. Merrimac, MA, Destiny Books, 1989.

Howells, Robert. *The Illuminati*. London, Watkins, 2016.

Kaplan, David E. and Marshall, Andrew. *The Cult at the End of the World*. New York, Crown, 1996.

Reston, James. *Dogs of God: Columbus, the Inquisition, and the Defeat of the Moors*. New York, Doubleday, 2005.

Ryan, Tom. *China Rising*. Collingwood, Victoria, HTAV, 2012.

Scheeres, Julia. *A Thousand Lives: The Untold Story of Jonestown*. New York, Free Press, 2011.

Wasserman, James. *An Illustrated History of The Knights Templar*. Merrimac, MA, Destiny Books, 2006.

Websites

Taiping Rebellion
http://taipingrebellion.com

Cielo Drive
http://www.cielodrive.com/charles-manson.php

Film

Witness To Waco. Directed by Faith Gaskins and Silvia Holmes Gaines. MSNBC, 2009.

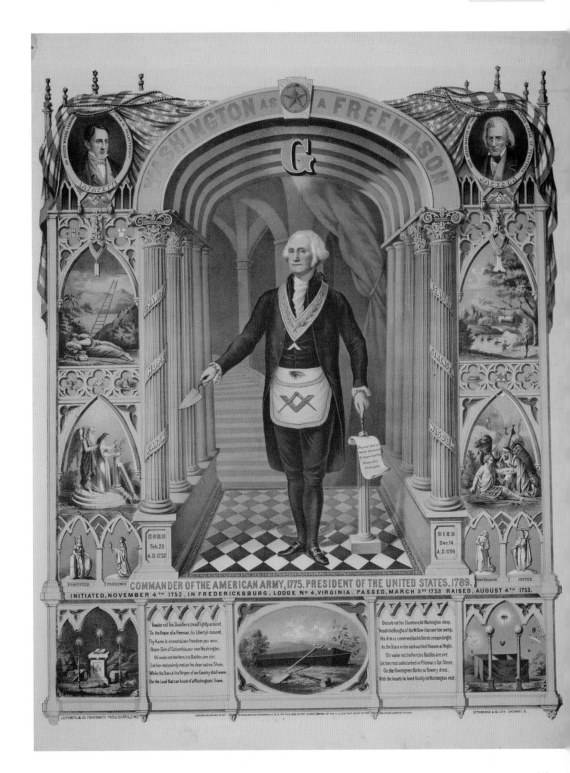

INDEX

Page numbers in **bold** refer to captions.

Picture Credits